· POPULAR ·
· COLLECTABLES ·

household
treasures

Muriel M. Miller

GUINNESS PUBLISHING

Dedication: *To Andrew, Catherine, David, and Rebecca who now have their own households.*

Project Editor: Honor Head
Editor: Beatrice Frei
Picture Research: Julie O'Leary
Design and Layout: Steve Leaning
Photographer: Peter Greenhalf

Published in Great Britain by
Guinness Publishing Ltd,
33 London Road, Enfield, Middlesex

Typeset in Caslon Old Face
by Ace Filmsetting Ltd, Frome
Printed and bound in Italy by
New Interlitho SpA, Milan

'Guinness' is a registered trade mark of
Guinness Superlatives Ltd

**British Library Cataloguing in
Publication Data**
Miller, Muriel M.
    Popular collectables, household
    treasures.
    1. Great Britain. Household objects,
    history
    I. Title
    643

    ISBN 0-85112-904-8

contents

FEATURES

introduction

Most of the items found in the home are so familiar that, inevitably, they are taken for granted – but many are the product of a fertile and inventive brain.

The vacuum cleaner that today is pushed across the carpet so effortlessly began life as a monstrous 'Puffing Billy', so large that it took a team of men to handle it.

Sewing machines were thought of as long ago as 1790, but it took almost another hundred years before they were fully developed for practical use – and then they were so expensive that a manufacturer, Isaac Singer, introduced a new and novel system of hire-purchase to make it easier for women to buy them.

The variety of collectable household items available can be bewildering and, for the beginner, it can be difficult to know where to start. Cookery books, for example, can be bought relatively cheaply, and they provide a fascinating insight into life as it was fifty or a hundred years ago. Then there are samplers. Used originally as teaching aids, they can be attractively framed to grace the home, but they can also be extremely expensive.

This book is intended to guide the novice through this fascinating and often intriguing world of domestic new inventions. Historical data is provided for interest, plus practical tips on what to look out for – and what to avoid. Brass warming pans, for example, were reproduced in great numbers during the 1970s and the inexperienced buyer can be easily deceived.

The subject matter covered in *Household Treasures* is necessarily diverse, ranging from hot water bottles to gramophones, foot scrapers to umbrellas, herb choppers to watch stands, and each item is dealt with in detail.

LEFT to RIGHT: Ceramic rolling pin; £16. Rolling pin in clear glass; £16. Both 20th century.
Three wooden rolling pins; £4–£8.

Stoneware storage jars with printed contents; £15–£20 each.

Hooked fireplace trivet in cast iron with a copper handle; £20–£30.

There are entries which describe how to recognise electroplated nickel silver and how not to confuse it with silver and what the difference is between close plate and Sheffield plate.

The book is arranged alphabetically for ease of reference, with a comprehensive glossary which explains some of the more unfamiliar terms. A table of registered design marks will enable the user to date metals, ceramics and glass.

Antiques fairs are good sources for buying and most dealers will readily guide and advise the beginner, but there are not many who specialise in household objects. Flea markets and car boot sales can provide unexpected bargains, however, and auctions, too, are well worth attending. It is essential to view carefully beforehand and check items for damage as, once the hammer has fallen, there can be no redress; the rule of *caveat emptor* (let the buyer beware) is rigidly upheld.

Whether you are starting a collection or building up an existing one, I hope *Household Treasures* adds to the excitement and fun. Happy hunting.

· APPLE · & · · CHEESE · · SCOOPS ·

These useful implements have been used since Roman times and scoops made of sheep shank bone are often excavated. The scoops are very similar in design to later apple corers, and are often incorrectly labelled as such.

The scoop would be inserted into the cheese, for example, given a slight twist and then withdrawn, bringing with it a sample of the cheese for tasting. Apple scoops were similarly employed but, it is maintained, were mainly used by the elderly who had lost their teeth and could not bite into the fruit.

Apple and cheese scoops were originally made of bone, and later of carved hardwood, ivory, and silver. The scoop, which varied in length between 3 to 6 inches (7½–15½ cm), could be made in one piece, being cut away along half its length into a narrow curved scoop shape. Alternatively, the scooped part was screwed on to a separate handle which, when unscrewed, could be reversed and slotted into the hollow

Three scoops, two in wood with metal grips and one in bone; £5–£15.

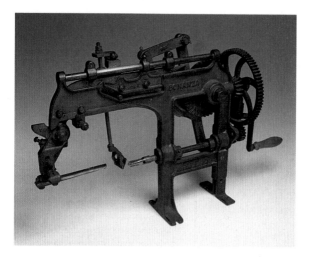

handle for storage and for use when
travelling. Wooden handles were either
plainly turned, or elaborately carved. A
plain bone scoop will be between £6–
£10.

'Bonanza' apple corer and
peeler, made by Goodell
& Co. Length 20 inches
(51 cm) (exc. handle),
height 15 inches (38 cm).

· APPLE ·
· PEELERS · & ·
· CORERS ·

The first machines for peeling and
coring apples appeared in the mid-19th
century. They were originally made of
cast iron, with aluminium being used
from about 1890. Large and rather
unwieldy, they were intended to be
screwed or clamped on to the kitchen
table.

The apple corer was hand-operated,
the handle rotating the corer, and also
driving a series of cog wheels which
were linked to a worm screw. This
screw operated the blades which peeled
the apple, so that the user cored and
peeled the apple in one simple
operation.

· BASKETS ·
WICKER

The definition of wicker is a small pliant twig or osier, and baskets have been made using willow and rushes since the Stone Age.

Baskets were woven in traditional shapes and styles which evolved either from the region where a certain produce was grown or manufactured, or because the basket was made to contain a particular item. Thus hop baskets were prevalent in Kent, and potato baskets were made in Lincolnshire; egg baskets were round, flower baskets long and flat in order to take the cut blooms. Rushes were used for making baskets that would contain soft fruit but, later, long soft willow shavings were used.

Baskets vary from being oblong with sloping sides, oval or tub-shaped, to being round with a narrowing top. Different weaves and varying colours of willow made it possible to give each basket an air of individuality.

Apart from being made to contain produce, baskets were made for a variety of domestic uses. Ladies would gather their flowers in a basket that consisted of a large woven 'disc' which was set on a wooden frame base before being drawn up into a shallow curved container by means of a solid wicker handle. Log baskets were deep tubs

Three traditional baskets showing the variety of colours and shapes used, £12–£15.

LEFT: 1930s basket decorated with raffia flowers, £12–£15.
RIGHT: Small laundry basket, £18–£20.

that were set beside the fireplace, while the washing was placed in a shallow oval laundry basket that had slanting sides and a small handle on each end.

Sewing and work baskets were square or round, and were lined with quilted silk in red or blue. Picnic hampers were large rectangular woven boxes, and were often fitted out with cups, saucers, plates, cutlery and, later, a vacuum flask, all held in place by means of leather straps.

Baskets were subjected to a great deal of use and those found today date from the late Victorian or Edwardian period and later. When buying a basket, ensure that the willow is not broken or damaged. Check also for woodworm. This can be treated, but if the basket is too far gone with worm, it is wiser to leave it alone.

Prices vary enormously depending on age, size and shape. Later baskets of a

LEFT to RIGHT: Flower trug, £12–£15; cherry picking basket, complete with hook, £20–£25; hamper with carrying handle £15–£20.

b

'shopping' style shape will cost about £5–£10 at auction, and an egg basket will be between £40–£60, depending on the pattern of the weave. A small sewing box with its original lining will cost about £25, while a fitted picnic basket will be around £50 upwards.

· BELLOWS ·
FIRE

Fire has been important to man since time immemorial, and fire bellows made from animal skins were used by the ancients to start a reluctant fire or revive the dying embers.

In countries with an inclement climate, which had the added difficulty of obtaining a flame before the advent of the tinder box, it was essential to keep the fire going twenty-four hours a day in the home. The fire was banked overnight and covered with a 'couvre-feu' or curfew, then in the morning the embers would be raked through and fanned into life.

Victorian bellows were usually made of two pieces or boards of shaped wood, held together by leather inserts. An inner coiled spring forced the bellows apart for the desired pumping action. The narrow nozzle was made of metal, either brass or iron. The wood was cut in a triangular or heart shape but, with the handles incorporated, the overall effect was that of the ace of spades as seen in a pack of cards.

Bellows covered with stamped sheet brass, £15–£20.

The wooden boards could be left plain, turned in a pattern of simple concentric circles, have an inlaid pattern, or be elaborately carved with fruit, flowers or foliage. Pokerwork patterns were often used, or designs picked out in tiny nails. Brass studs were also added for extra decoration. Alternatively, the boards could be covered with plush or velvet, or by a sheet of hammered or stamped brass or copper.

When buying, care should be taken that the leather is still sound, and that the nozzle is not a replacement. Any plush covering should still have its nap and not be too worn. Reproduction bellows can be mistaken for the real thing, but the brass on these is thin and too bright. The price also reflects their age and they can be bought for about £8–£12.

Bellows can still be bought cheaply at auction, and a fairly plain example with a pokerwork design will cost about £15–£30. Plush examples will be about £25–£50. Bellows with a stamped brass finish of ornate design will be about £50–£100.

Group of fire bellows in wood and brass, £20–£90.

· BISCUIT ·
· MOULDS · & ·
· CUTTERS ·

Wooden moulds for creating various patterns and shapes in biscuit making were usually carved from a single piece of wood. These 'cards', as they were known, could be square or rectangular, and ranged in thickness from between half an inch to just over one inch (1½–2½ cm). Patterns were often carved on both sides and were many and varied.

Favourite biscuits were shortbread, and a spicy ginger biscuit known nowadays as gingerbread. The uncooked biscuit mixture would be pressed into the mould, then gently eased out before being baked. Sometimes the pattern was pressed on before cooking by means of a wooden rolling pin (q.v.). The main ingredient for an early 17th-century gingerbread was breadcrumbs; eggs, fat or flour not being used. The mixture was pre-cooked by boiling and not baked.

Motifs on the cards varied widely, and included animals such as dogs, horses, sheep and pigs, birds such as swans, rural scenes showing windmills or castles, Biblical characters such as Moses, and nursery rhyme characters like Puss in Boots. Apples, pears and wheatsheaves were depicted, as were Punch and Judy, angels, and historical personages. Alphabet biscuits were made in gingerbread and decorated with edible gold leaf in order to encourage children with their reading and writing.

By the 19th century, mechanisation had made it possible to mass-produce biscuit cutters in tin. The gingerbread man made his appearance, as did serrated circles, stars, crescents and hearts, various animals, and initial letters. Sets of cutters with plain or

Two wooden biscuit moulds showing cottages and a thistle; £50–£100.

Selection of Victorian moulds and cutters, £5–£50.

fluted edges were of escalating size and were designed to fit one inside the other.

Prices vary enormously according to the size and design of the mould, but generally fall between about £50–£100 each.

· BISCUIT ·
· TINS ·

The theory that attractive or eye-catching packaging helped sell the product became widespread in the 19th century, and among the pioneers were Huntley & Palmer, famous biscuit makers. Their biscuits had been sold in tins since the 1820s, but these were plain, being embellished only by a paper label glued on to the outside. In 1868, Huntley's son, Joseph, who ran an ironmongery and tin-making business under the name of Huntley, Boorne & Stevens, began supplying his father with tins.

At first, the tins were decorated with transfer printing, but in 1872 the firm of Barclay and Fry patented a method of offset lithography printing which enabled a variety of surfaces to be colour printed. This patent was sold to Bryant and May who allowed Huntley,

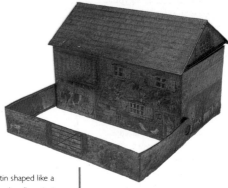

Biscuit tin shaped like a farm, the handle swinging down to form the perimeter 'hedge'.

Boorne & Stevens extensive rights to the new process until the patent ran out in 1888. Huntley, Boorne & Stevens were to amalgamate with Bryant & May and Hudson Scott to form the Allied Tin Box Makers in 1921, and later became known as the Metal Box Company.

The new process allowed curved and shaped surfaces to be decorated, and so biscuit tins were made in novel shapes up until the late 1930s. Manufacturers such as Huntley & Palmer, Jacob's, Peek Frean, and Crawford's intended them as gifts or issued them for sale at Christmas, and some of these can be dated. Tins that could be used afterwards as children's toys were extremely popular, and these can be found modelled as prams, windmills, cars, grandfather clocks, sentry boxes, gypsy caravans, world globes, cannons, and the Gold State Coach coach.

Some tins were extremely decorative, such as a box made in imitation of Persian papier mâché, or could be shaped as goldfish bowls, complete with painted fish and lilies, powder compacts (which held tiny 'iced gems' from Crawford's), handbags, both 'leather' and 'woven', a briefcase, an Egyptian urn decorated with coloured geometric designs, a revolving-style bookcase, complete with shelves of painted books, single individual books seemingly bound in gold-tooled leather, and a gilded 'veneered' chest of drawers in 18th-century style.

Not all tins were of novel shape, however, with some relying on decorative transfer printing for appeal. Pre-Raphaelite paintings were reproduced in careful detail, as were romantic 18th-century scenes. Cavalry officers from the Boer War were shown on the sides of an octagonal tin. Oval and rectangular tins were decorated with sprays or garlands of flowers, as were square-sided upright containers. Jacob's packaged their famous 'Cream Crackers' in chunky oblong tins which had imitation wood veneer.

Biscuit tins of novel shape are the most collectable. They are more desirable in good condition, and not scratched, worn, or dented. Any damage will affect the price. A litho-decorated tin should be cleaned with cotton wool that is barely damp, and that has been dabbed with good quality soap, to get rid of dirt. It should then be dried by placing in a warm oven at very low heat, before polishing with plain clear white wax (not a silicone polish). When dry and hard, it can be polished with a soft cloth. Many boxes are stamped underneath with the biscuit maker's name.

Prices can be high, with the Coronation coach costing about £200 upwards; a Jacob's houseboat will be £100–£150. A tin in the style of a Japanese porcelain vase will be about £50–£100. Plainly-shaped tins will start at about £10–£20 upwards depending on the pattern on the lid.

·BLANKET·
·BOXES·

The origins of the wooden blanket box can be traced back to the flat-topped planked coffer or board chest of the Middle Ages. This was made of plain planks of wood and the lid was held to the base by heavy metal pin or strap hinges. The coffer was kept closed by means of an iron lock and hasp. Despite the later construction of joined or framed chests with inset panels, planked chests were still being made in the 1800s.

In the 16th and 17th centuries, chests were used as storage boxes for clothes. They were made mainly in oak, although the rich also had them made in cypress, a wood which repelled moths. Later 18th-century chests were also made in cedarwood, also moth-repellent, or had cedarwood linings.

In the mid-19th century, the coffer saw a revival when the Victorians reproduced the Tudor-style chest. These were made by using new 'antiqued' wood, or by incorporating genuine antique panels which could be 'improved' by additional carving or inlaying. Turn-of-the-century chests were set on short legs and were decorated with ribbed panels in

Oak blanket box with dove-tailed corners and an interior lidded candle box. Length 25 inches (63.5 cm), width 20 inches (51 cm), height 11 inches (28 cm); £75–£80.

Domed pine box c.1860.
Length 20 inches (51 cm),
width 12 inches (30.5
cm), height 12 inches
(30.5 cm); £75–£100.

imitation of linenfold carving. These
were known as hall chests and were
intended for storage of travelling rugs or
blankets.

Despite the term 'blanket chest'
which originated in the 18th century,
the chests were used mainly for storage
of clothes or treasured possessions. A
small inner box or drawer was often
incorporated into boxes made of pine.
This is known as a candle box and did,
in fact, contain candles. The candles
were used as a moth repellent.

Pine chests were left plain, or could
be ornamented by painting. Simple
inlay designs were painted on the
outside and the inner lid. Seamen's
chests would be decorated on the inside
of the lid with appropriate pictures.
They were rarely painted on the
outside, as this would be damaged by
the frequent transportation of the chest.

Domed chests were also popular with
the Victorians. These often had wood
and metal strapping and metal carrying
handles. Alternatively, they could be
leather bound with wooden splats for
decoration.

When buying chests, care must be
taken as they are often restored or made
up from old wood. The lid tended to
split over the years, so check that this is
original. Check for woodworm; this
can be treated but if it is extensive, then it
will devalue the chest. Hand-painting is

Pine chest with metal corners c.1860, marked 'Burne British Manufacture'. Length 20 inches (51 cm), width 13 inches (33 cm), height 12 inches (30.5 cm); £75–£100.

often a modern addition, especially that on seamen's chests. Pine chests were sometimes over-painted, but these can be 'stripped' to the wood, sanded and polished.

Early reproduction oak chests made in the Victorian era, well designed and with a great deal of carving, are expensive and will cost between about £300–£700 upwards. A hall chest made in about 1900 will be £100–£150. Pine chests, on the other hand, are cheaper to buy and easier to find. A plain chest will start at about £100–£200, as will a domed chest with metal strapping.

· BOOT · & · · SHOE · TREES ·

These wooden items came into fashion some time in the 19th century, and it was part of a valet's duties to ensure that a pair of trees was slipped into his master's shoes as soon as they were

Selection of shoe trees made in sycamore wood; £8–£10.

taken off. The trees were designed to keep the boot or shoe in shape by raising the forepart into a foot shape, which prevented the leather from cracking.

The trees were usually made in beechwood, although other woods, such as pinewood, were also occasionally used. Some trees were intended to fill the shoe completely and were jointed halfway down to facilitate insertion into the footwear. These have a large knobbed handle set into the heel. Adjustable trees of this kind were lengthened at the joint by means of a 'mousetrap' type of lever which was set into the heel. Half trees merely had the form of the front part of the foot and were inserted by means of a metal grip.

'Watt's Patent Tree' was an adjustable tree, and was available from about 1880. It was simply made and consisted of a very narrow foot shape which could be raised or lowered, shortened or elongated, by means of a threaded crosspiece. An instep stretcher was also available and this consisted of a flattish wooden sole to which was attached a wooden foot form. This could also be raised or lowered by twisting a large threaded spindle, thus gently stretching the leather to accommodate the wearer's foot more comfortably. There were also stretchers which would widen the shoe.

Simple shoe trees in the form of a wooden toe-cap attached to a springy strip of metal with a wooden heel date from the 1920–30s.

Boot and shoe trees are often found at flea markets and car boot sales where they can be bought cheaply for only a few pounds or even less. If sold by a specialist dealer, they will be dearer, and a man's foot-shaped tree will be about £10 upwards.

Group of adjustable shoe trees; £8–£10.

b

· BOOTSCRAPERS ·
· & · FOOT ·
· WIPERS ·

Cast iron bootscrapers, popular with the Victorians and Edwardians, were set outside the back or front door of a house and were used to scrape the mud and dirt from boots and shoes before the wearer entered the establishment. They had been in use since the 18th century, but with the development of new techniques in the Victorian era, especially around the Coalbrookdale area, all manner of cast iron items, including bootscrapers, were capable of being finely moulded in intricate and novel shapes.

The basic requirement of a good scraper was a stout bar or blade that could be used to scrape off the mud. The simplest design had several blades set in a horizontal grid-like arrangement and was generally for outdoor use, as the scraped-off mud would fall between the blades and on to the ground. Other scrapers intended for outdoor use consisted of a single bar, set on vertical supports and fixed immovably into the paving stone or doorstep.

Two cast iron bootscrapers.
ABOVE £50–£100.
BELOW £25–£50.

The pan scraper had a single horizontal blade that was supported by a central column. This column was often ornately cast, and could be lyre shaped with attractive scroll decoration. Alternatively, the blade could be suspended between two pillar-like supports, or set in an upturned horseshoe shape. The pan itself was also decorative, being edged with scrolls or shell-shapes, or it could be curved or lobed. The falling mud from the boot would rest in the pan to be later cleared away, and this type was often set just inside the door, in the hallway or lobby.

Boot and shoe wipers involved the

addition of a brush or brushes which did the job of thoroughly cleaning the dirty footwear. The iron-framed 'New Walrond' combined a scraper with an angled toe brush, while the 'Major Bootscraper and Wiper' had revolving cylinder brushes and steel wire scrapers. Revolving cleaners without scrapers were used in 'David's Patent Rollermat', and this had rollers covered with coconut-fibre mats. Long-handled bristle brushes were also used for cleaning the mud off boots.

Cast iron boot scrapers are surprisingly collectable and can fetch high prices. Any rust can be removed by using a stiff wire brush, although it should be avoided if the surface is too badly pitted. The scraper can then be polished up by using a proprietary grate polish, available from an ironmongers.

Simple grid-style scrapers will be about £20–£50, while the more ornate pan scrapers will start at about £100.

'Hedgehog' boot cleaner and scraper. Height 38 inches (96.5 cm), width 25 inches (63.5 cm); £60.

· BOTTLE ·
· OPENERS ·

The bottle opener first came into being with the invention of the Codd bottle, a mineral water bottle invented by Hiram Codd in 1870. The bottle was sealed by means of a built-in glass 'marble' in the neck. This was kept in position under the pressure of the gas in the bottle. The marble was released for pouring by being pressed down with a wooden cup which contained a slim projection or plunger.

When the Crown Cork Company produced a crimped metal and cork cap in 1892, which clamped firmly on to the neck of the bottle, the Crown cork opener was invented. This consisted either of a hooked arrangement which enabled the metal cap to be eased off the bottle, or of a rounded triangle of metal with a narrow inner flange for opening.

Some openers were plainly made of metal or cast iron. Many of these were used for advertising purposes and were stamped or embossed with the name of the drinks' retailer, or the manufacturer of the contents of the bottle. Novelty openers could be made in many designs, in the shape of a bottle of beer, or perhaps fashioned like a key.

Prices are varied, depending on the style of the bottle opener. Advertising openers start at about £1–£2; those of more interesting shape will be about £5 upwards.

· BREAD · BOARDS · · & · KNIVES ·

These round flat wooden boards were used when cutting loaves of bread, and have been made from the Victorian era onwards.

The edges of these bread boards are often ornately carved. Motifs such as leaves, flowers or ears of corn were frequently used, together with the word 'Bread' carved in Gothic script, or mottoes such as 'The Staff of Life', 'Be Thankful' or 'Our Daily Bread'. Messages such as 'Long Life and

LEFT: Bread board with a carving of fruit and leaves; £20–£30.
RIGHT: An octagonal board with a decoration of carved leaves and flowers; £20–£30.

LEFT: Bread board carved with the motto 'Long Life and Happiness', intended as a wedding present; £25–£35.
RIGHT: Commemorative board celebrating Queen Victoria's Diamond Jubilee 1837–1897; £30–£35.

Happiness' were carved on bread boards intended as wedding gifts.

Bread knives were made with blades of Sheffield steel which could be smoothed or serrated. The handles were made of wood and ornately carved, or could be of silver, silver plate, or ivory. Scrolls or wheat ears were favourite decorations.

It is possible to clean stained bread boards by scrubbing with an abrasive powder, but it is best to leave badly marked boards alone as some stains prove stubborn. They can then be buffed up with a good quality beeswax polish, if wanted for decorative purposes. Prices vary between about £20–£35, depending on the amount of carving and the rarity of the motto.

Selection of bread knives with wooden, porcelain and silver-plated handles; £20–£30.

Bread knives also cost about £20–£35 if in good condition. Rust can be removed by rubbing with very fine grade wire wool, but avoid blades that are badly pitted, or very worn with use.

· BRITANNIA · · METAL ·

This was a new alloy of tin, brass, copper, antimony and bismuth, developed in 1770. It was capable of taking a high polish and was made in order to compete with Sheffield plate (q.v.). At first it was known as white metal, receiving the name 'Britannia Metal' in about 1797.

The first manufacturer appears to be James Vickers of Sheffield, who confined his initial output to spoons and forks, later producing items such as small boxes, candlesticks, and so on. However, the largest producer of Britannia metal wares was James Dixon & Sons of Sheffield.

Britannia metal achieved a dull grey patina over the years, particularly that which was made before the mid-19th century, and it can be confused with pewter. However, unlike pewter, Britannia metal contains no lead, and is therefore harder, not so prone to deep scratches. It will also resist careful pressure from the hands, unlike pewter which tends to 'give'. The metal can be buffed to a high shine, but collectors will often prefer the sign of age.

A hinged Britannia metal food mould in the shape of a fish.

· BUTTER · STAMPS ·
· MOULDS · & ·
· BATS ·

After the cream was separated from the milk, it was poured into a wooden churn and then agitated to make butter. Some churns had a perforated plunger which had to be thrust up and down vigorously. Other churns were set on rockers and could be foot-operated. The paddle box developed into the 'end-over-end' churn. This was barrel-like in shape and was rotated over and over, using a handle.

Pair of ribbed wooden butter bats; £10–£20.

After the butter had 'come', the excess moisture was squeezed out and it was placed on a table to be worked on with a pair of butter bats which removed any remaining water. The bats, also known as scotch hands, were made of wood, plain on one side and with a zig-zag or ribbed pattern on the other. The butter was worked rapidly and shaped into balls or squares. It was then ready for stamping decoratively.

The carved wooden butter stamp or print had originally been used by the dairy farmer as his trademark when selling the butter at the market, but by the mid-19th century, butter was stamped decoratively for use on the table. The print was often fitted with a handle or knob for ease of use and each block of butter was quickly stamped. Butter rollers were also used, and these consisted of a carved wooden roller which was set between two knobbed, wooden prongs. This was then drawn along the surface of the butter, producing an attractive repeat pattern.

Butter prints, £50–£70 each.

Butter moulds were also used. The carved stamp was set into a container, the butter pressed in firmly, then ejected by means of a plunger. Alternatively, a two-part mould was

b

Group of butter stamps
and a butter mould;
£40–£60.

used, with a mirror-image pattern on
each piece.

Carved patterns were related to the
countryside. Flowers, leaves and birds,
such as the swan, were hand-carved in
stylised form. Some farmers used a cow
as if to emphasise the quality of their
butter. In Scotland the thistle was a
favourite motif, while in England the
rose was used.

Plain ribbed butter bats will cost
about £10–£20; later bats from about
1920 will cost between £4–£6. Butter
prints around 3½ inches (9 cm) in
diameter will be about £50–£100 each;
those of larger size are over £100. Butter
rollers with a simple leaf design will also
be £50–£100.

· BUTTONHOOKS ·
· & · SHOEHORNS ·

These two items, although at first sight
totally unrelated, are often classified
together, partly because they were both
used on footwear, and partly because
they were often sold together as part of
a lady's dressing set.

Although buttonhooks had been used prior to the Victorian era, the change in fashion dictated that they should become an essential part of everyday life. Dresses were now made with endless rows of tiny buttons, and the hook made life easier. Long buttoned kid gloves were *de rigueur* and tiny buttonhooks were made specifically for these. By 1880, soft kid shoes had given way to tougher high-buttoned leather shoes which were difficult to fasten.

The buttonhook was also used by men for fastening their riding boots or gaiters.

The cheapest buttonhooks were made in steel and were sometimes part of the all-purpose pocket implement that incorporated a bottle opener and a miniature screwdriver. Sometimes the hooks were set in a 'slide' action case that also held a pencil and penknife, or they could form part of a penknife that had implements other than just a blade.

Selection of buttonhooks; £5–£15.

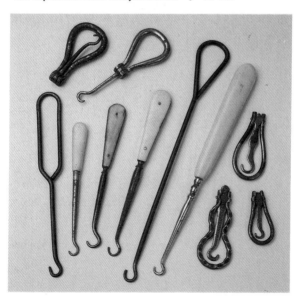

Combined buttonhooks
and shoehorns.
LEFT to RIGHT:
15 inches (38 cm),
11 inches (28 cm),
9 inches (23 cm) in
length; £5–£10.

Long flexible wooden
shoe horn with a swan's
head handle. Length 18
inches (45.7 cm).

Plain fold-over hooks were intended for pocket use, the hook folding snugly into the looped handle.

Cast metal hooks with plain looped handles were often given away by retailers and these were embossed with the name of the shop or store.

Buttonhooks with fanciful handles abounded. *Risqué* handles made in the form of a female leg were a favourite motif with Victorian men, who seldom saw even an ankle. Novelty handles featured birds such as swans, herons, parrots and owls; animals such as dogs, lions and elephants, and these were sometimes adorned with jewelled eyes. Characters such as a jester, teddy bear or Mr Punch vied with heads of negroes.

The Victorians' passion for travel led to souvenir buttonhooks, the metal heads bearing the crest or symbol of the resort or county. Natural stones such as agate or carved jet were used for the handles and these were also sold at seaside resorts. Tortoiseshell, ebony, bone, ivory and amber were other natural materials that were used extensively. Mother-of-pearl handles were carved in 'candle-end' or 'featherhead' designs.

Silver-handled buttonhooks were usually part of a dressing set and these were made between about 1860–1914. Although the average length was between 7 and 9 inches (18–23 cm), they could vary in size from a tiny hook under 1 inch (2½ cm) long, used for gloves, to a giant example over 18 inches (46 cm) long which would have been used by ladies who found bending difficult. The handles could be plain, have figural heads, or they could be attractively embossed in a seemingly infinite number of different designs, such as scrolling, feather patterns, or stamped with winged cherubs' heads.

Shoehorns were intended to ease the tight-fitting boot or shoe on to the foot without hurting the wearer and without causing damage to the back of the shoe. They were regarded as much a part of the dressing set as the buttonhook and the style, design and pattern of the handle was often identical. They were sometimes combined in one article, the shoehorn being made of ivory and used as a handle for the steel hook. Sometimes encased in leather holders, they were known as the ladies' purse or pocket companions. Other combination sets had the hook set on a swivel, which folded neatly for pocket use.

When buying buttonhooks check that those with silver handles are firmly set with their steel hook. Handles taken from cutlery have sometimes been used as replacements. Avoid examples where the silver is worn and thin, split or badly dented. The steel hook is prone to rust but this can be removed by rubbing with a fine grade steel wool.

Plain, small buttonhooks start at about £5–£10 and those with carved mother-of-pearl handles are about the same price. Advertising hooks cost about £10–£20, while those with handles made in natural stone are £20–£25. Silver-handled buttonhooks vary in price according to size, and will be about £20–£28.

Shoehorns are usually slightly cheaper than buttonhooks, although much depends on the style of the handle.

Group of shoehorns made of copper, horn, ebony, silver (handle only), and base metal; £4–£15.

Two Worcester extinguishers, caricaturing the singer Jenny Lind, who was known as the 'Swedish Nightingale'; £600–£700 the pair.

Four Worcester extinguishers.
LEFT to RIGHT:
'Mob Cap' (1879), £500;
'Old Lady' (1881), £450;
'Budge' (1893), £400;
'Toddie' (1892), £450.

· CANDLE ·
· EXTINGUISHERS ·

The self-consuming wick which could be blown out in safety had been invented by about 1830, so that the extinguisher was already redundant by the time it first went into production in the 1850s. The ceramic candle extinguishers were therefore ornamental rather than practical. They were hollow, usually conical in shape, rather like a dunce's cap, and were made both with and without a handle.

Early candle extinguishers were made by Royal Crown Derby between about 1848–1935, and in huge quantities by Royal Worcester in the short period from 1870 to 1880. Extinguishers were also produced by W. H. Goss between 1862–1944, and crested examples were made by factories such as Arkinstall & Sons (Arcadian China) 1904–1924.

Some extinguishers were bell shaped and had their own tray or stand, while Goss produced examples resembling a trumpet, a witch's hat, and a Welsh steeple hat. The nightcap with its dunce's hat shape was also frequently used and one can find owls and dogs wearing this. Figures, both human and animal, were popular, as were heads. Worcester are credited with providing

Four Worcester
extinguishers.
LEFT to RIGHT:
'Hush' (1924), £400;
'Monsieur Reynard'
(1928), £220;
'Mandarin' (1917), £120;
'Geisha' (1921), £120.

some of the most interesting designs
and they made extinguishers in the form
of a nun, a monk, a Chinese girl, a
mandarin, and various others. They also
portrayed real people and Jenny Lind
appeared in two versions. Arcadian
China produced a suffragette.

Extinguishers are still being made,
using the original moulds, and if these
are examined where they are sold in
good quality shops, it will help with
identifying and differentiating between
old and new. Collectors should also be
familiar with the makers' marks
stamped on by factories such as Royal
Worcester and Derby, as this will help
with dating.

Prices for marked extinguishers are
high and vary between about £50–£100
depending on the subject, with more
exotic extinguishers costing much more.

· CANDLE ·
· SNUFFERS ·
& WICK TRIMMERS

Before the invention of the self-
consuming wick in about 1830, candle
wicks were made of loosely plaited
cotton and had a dangerous tendency
to curl over and fall into the molten
tallow as they burned, causing the
candle to splutter and smoke badly. A
more major hazard was that the wick
might break off and fall, still
smouldering, on to the table. The
householder therefore used a scissors-

Early wick trimmers and
candleholders.

C

like snuffer to trim the wick to a safer and more manageable length. When the wick was cut, it fell into a box-like arrangement that was attached to one of the blades of the wick trimmer, and was contained there in safety. At the end of the day, a scissor-like implement with flat, spade-like end plates was used to put out the candle, and this was called a douter.

Victorian wick trimmers stood on small feet, and were made of metal, such as Britannia metal (q.v.), pewter, brass, iron and steel, the latter sometimes having silver-mounted handles and finger grips. They are usually found alone, or with a matching tray which could be attractively scrolled or have pierced borders. Some smaller snuffers were intended to be kept with the chamberstick and slotted in place, being securely held by means of a metal peg set under the lower blade. The box-like arrangement for containing the wick was generally rectangular, sometimes square, oval, or barrel-shaped.

Occasionally, snuffers can be found with curved open pans rather than boxes, and these were set at the sides of the blades. The scissors always had pointed ends and these were used to

Steel candle snuffers and wick trimmers; £20–£30

32

Silver-plated snuffers with ornate finger grips.

prise the cooled and solidified wax out of the candlestick.

Large-sized snuffers could be equipped with a mechanical blade and were called eccentric trimmers. The blade was sprung and held the wick in place in the box.

When buying candle snuffers, these should be checked for wear on the scissor mechanism and on the hinges. Check that the feet are original and not replacements; avoid those with missing feet unless they are 18th-century examples, which had no feet. Silver-mounted handles have a hallmark (q.v.) on the finger grips and this will date the trimmers. The mechanism of eccentric snuffers should also be checked, as repairs are expensive.

Prices can be very high for early examples and those of eccentric style and will be between £200–£400. However, later trimmers of plain design, made in steel, can be bought at auction for anything from about £20–£30 upwards; if complete with a silver-plated tray, they will start at £40–£50.

TOP: Snuffers with spring-loaded closure.
BOTTOM: Snuffers with 'lift-up' side and box. Marked with a crown and 'V.R. Patented'.

C

· CANDLESTICKS ·
CHAMBERSTICKS & HOLDERS

The earliest type of candlestick, used in
about 3000 BC. consisted of a spike on
to which the candle was set firmly. By
the 10th century, candlesticks were
made for use in churches and
monasteries and by the 15th century
were being used in the home.

The Victorian era saw the dawn of
mechanisation and almost every
domestic item was mass-produced.
Candlesticks were made in all manner
of materials: silver, brass, pewter, silver-
plate, wood, porcelain, pottery and glass.

Brass was perhaps the favourite metal
with the working classes and styles
imitated those of the more expensive
silver sticks found in the rich man's
home. Candlesticks from earlier periods
were copied in plain, Baroque and
Rococo style, had knopped columns set
on square or round bases, or had barley
sugar twist columns set on circular
bases. Sometimes there was a metal
prick set into the nozzle. This was
attached to a long rod that extended
through the column of the candlestick,
and had a twofold purpose. The candle
could be pushed well down into the

Selection of single brass
candlesticks, £10–£40
each, £25–£100 in pairs.

C

Group of chambersticks in pottery, glass, brass and silver-plate; £10–£35.

stick for safety and pushed up using the rod as it gradually burned down. It also enabled the candle to be firmly fixed in the nozzle.

Chambersticks were squat versions of the candlestick, having a large integral drip pan and a carrying handle. They were generally for bedroom use and the pan caught any drips that occurred when the user was lighting his way to bed. Occasionally, a small cone-shaped extinguisher (see CANDLE EXTINGUISHERS) was attached to the side of the tray for snuffing out the candle. The chambersticks were made in brass, iron, enamelled metal, wood, pottery and porcelain.

Multi-branched candelabra were used for lighting the table or for placing on the sideboard. These were nearly always silver-plated and often had fluted columns in the Corinthian style. The arms which supported the nozzles were sometimes ribbed, and looped or twisted halfway along their length.

Glassmaking had also been mechanised and press-moulded glass made its appearance in the latter half of the 19th century. Candlesticks were made in a variety of colours such as red,

Glass candle and chambersticks; £5–£20.

blue, an oily green-yellow, dark green and amber, and marbled glass in amethyst, green and blue. Clear glass sticks, pressed in intricate patterns which imitated the more expensive cut glass, brilliantly reflected the light. These varied from plain ribbed columns set on stepped, petal feet to baluster shapes with basketwork feet.

Pottery and porcelain candlesticks were also popular and could be of plain style, decorated with transfer-printed designs, or could be extremely ornate with winged cherubs clinging to the column and garlands of flowers winding their way up the nozzles. Some candlesticks came with the metal pricks used in the brass varieties.

Despite the advent of electricity, candlesticks were still being manufactured in the 1920s/1930s. Glass candlesticks were made in frosted glass, the nozzles supported by half-clad females. Two-branched sticks were made in angular stepped fashion. Pottery and porcelain holders were squat, relying on painted or transfer-printed decoration for appeal. Colours were vivid, with strong orange, flame red and bright yellow being favourite. Patterns were very definite and consisted of stylised flower-heads or bold geometric designs.

Brass candlesticks are still being made today, and in the Victorian style, so it is important to recognise a reproduction. Victorian brass was generally paler than that made nowadays, and less 'brassy' in appearance. Modern brass can be 'distressed' by denting and scratching it in an effort to simulate age. It should therefore be carefully examined. Check the underside for newness of casting, and also check any screws that might be present. Ensure that there is no welding or soldering on old sticks. If the candlesticks are silver-plated, ensure that the plating is not yellowed or worn thin.

China cherub-style candlesticks decorated with flowers and foliage should be carefully checked for damage to leaves and blossoms. Chips and cracks in ornate pressed glass do not

LEFT to RIGHT: Wooden candlestick, £25–£30. One of a pair of pottery sticks, £20–£25 the pair. Wooden barley twist stick, £15–£20. Watcombe pottery candlestick, £40–£50. Wooden barley twist stick, £15–£20.

always show up. Examine the sticks with the eyes closed, as chips are often felt rather than seen.

Prices for brass candlesticks start at about £20–£25 for a single. Pairs are more than twice the price and will start from £60–£80. Victorian chambersticks in enamel will cost from about £10; brass from about £20. Bracket sticks for use on pianos can be found surprisingly cheaply at auction. They are frequently dulled with age and the intricate designs can be difficult to clean, which perhaps discourages prospective buyers. Prices will start at about £10–£15 for a single; £25 upwards for pairs.

A china candlestick will start at about £10–£15 for a single, about £20–£30 for a pair, but much depends on the style and pattern, and the manufacturer's collectability.

· CARPET ·
· SWEEPERS ·

The first mechanical means of keeping a carpet free of dirt and fluff was patented in 1853. It was of simple design and contained a brush inside a box which revolved by means of string attached to a pulley. A later version had two cast iron rollers plus the brush and this was operated by a belt-driven pulley attached to the rear roller.

In the 1870s an American, Melville R. Bissell, designed a wooden-bodied carpet sweeper that had spiralling rows of brushes and was friction driven by four rubber-covered wheels. It was emptied by means of a lever which opened and closed the dust box. Other models had side brushes for dealing with skirting boards, and the height of the spiralling brushes could be adjusted to suit all carpets.

The cleaner was an immediate success and its manufacture led to the formation of the Bissell Carpet Sweeper Company. The 'Grand Rapids' model of about 1895 is very similar to carpet sweepers found today and had rubber furniture guards or 'bumpers'. By the turn of the century, Bissell were producing a three-quarter-sized sweeper 'suitable for ladies' which retailed at ten shillings and sixpence (52½ pence) and even made toy sweepers called 'The Baby' and 'Little Jewel'. These cost ninepence ha'penny (approximately four pence) and two shillings and eightpence (about 13 pence) respectively.

Ewbank Ltd were British manufacturers of carpet sweepers and they produced the 'Ewbank Royal', costing twelve shillings and sixpence (62½ pence) in 1907, and the 'Ewbank Success' at ten shillings and sixpence (52½ pence) in 1911.

Carpet sweepers are not readily available at antiques fairs and the best place to look for them is at car boot sales or small auction sales. Prices will vary according to age and condition, but an early Ewbank in fine condition can be £50 or more.

(See also VACUUM CLEANERS.)

'Grand Rapids' carpet sweeper made by Bissell c.1895.

chamber pots

The invention of the first chamber pot is generally attributed to the Sybarites, Greek colonists who settled in Italy in around 720 BC. These early pots were boat shaped and the familiar rounded chamber pot did not make its appearance in Europe until medieval times, although the oblong pot retained its popularity in France until the early 19th century.

Chamber pots were made in various materials: china and pottery, terracotta, pewter, silver-plate, and silver. Earthenware examples have been found which date from the 17th century and these are slightly taller than their 18th- and 19th-century counterparts.

Despite the invention of the water closet early in Victoria's reign, most people still kept a supply of chamber pots in the house. Although they were used mainly in the bedroom or 'chamber' where they were kept in a pot cupboard or under the bed, a practice which gave rise to the nickname 'guzunder', they were also used elsewhere. After dinner, the gentlemen guests would stay in the dining room or retire to the smoking room to sample their host's port, and chamber pots were available in both rooms for their comfort. The pots were discreetly hidden in a cupboard or in a larger commode which was designed to look as much like a piece of furniture as possible. Alternatively, they could be tucked away in a purpose-built cupboard concealed in the panelling.

The oblong pot favoured by the French was also intended for discreet use. This was termed a *bourdalou*, the name being derived from that of a French Jesuit preacher, popular in the 17th century, who was noted for the length of his sermons. The ladies of the time had been obliged to carry with them a chamber pot which was

LEFT: Lidded chamber pot in puce transfer-printed design c.1880; £180–£200.
TOP RIGHT: Blue and white transfer-printed pot; £30–£60.
BOTTOM RIGHT: Blue and white transfer-printed bourdalou; £300–£500.

slipped under their voluminous dresses when the need arose. It was also used on long journeys, when it was known as a 'coach pot', and later, when hooped skirts became fashionable, it became known as a 'crinoline slipper'.

Chamber pots were ideal vehicles for insult. Notables of the day,

CHAMBER POTS   *TOP to BOTTOM*

LEFT: Carlton ware pot with gilded and enamelled decoration; £80–£120. *RIGHT*: Royal Torquay Pottery chamber pot; £60–£100.

Two Victorian chamber pots, the one with the blue bow made by Bishop & Stonier c.1880. *LEFT*: £50–£80. *RIGHT*: £30–£40.

LEFT: Blue lustre chamber pot 'Appleland' by Grimwades; £60–£75. *RIGHT*: Fine china pot by Hammersley; £60–£85.

chamber pots

such as Napoleon Bonaparte and George III, were featured on both the outside and inside, and even as late as the 1940s, pots could be found with a portrait of Adolf Hitler on the inside with the message to 'Have this on "old nasty"'.

Humorous and vulgar pots carried messages such as 'Oh landlord, fill the flowing bowl', or had a realistic ceramic frog sitting inside. Arthur Wood's factory produced a pot called 'The Anti-Splash Thunder Bowl' and this came complete with a large staring eye on the interior base.

Chamber pots were popular as wedding gifts. They could be two-handled, and carry the motto, 'Pass it this way, my dear' or perhaps. 'Use me well and keep me clean, and I will not tell what I have seen'. Three-handled pots were also made, as well as lidded pots; musical pots played a tune when lifted up.

Chamber pots have become very collectable and those of rare design will be expensive. Plain white pots can be found for about £3 or £4, and those with a simple transfer-printed pattern will be about £10 upwards; a more ornately patterned pot will be between about £60-£80. Blue and white transfer printed chamber pots will cost about £40-£100 upwards, while those with mottoes will start at about £150-£180. An oblong *bourdalou* will be at least £250 or more.

TOP: A four-handled marriage pot bearing the motto, 'Hand it over to me, my dear'; £200-£250. LEFT: Victorian version of an earlier marriage pot with a verse on both front and back and an interior caricature; £120-£180. RIGHT: A musical chamber pot which plays when lifted. Made by Crown Devon and called 'The Anti-Splash Thunder Bowl'; £100-£150.

· CHARCOAL ·
· IRONS ·
See Irons

· CLOSE ·
· PLATING ·

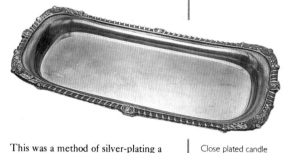

Close plated candle
snuffer tray c.1820.

This was a method of silver-plating a
finished object made of iron or steel.
The object to be treated was cleaned
and prepared before being dipped in a
solution of sal-ammoniac. It was then
coated or dipped into a molten liquid
solder that was tin based, and which
acted as a flux. A thin sheet of silver foil
was laid on to the surface of the piece
and hammered or pressed firmly into
place. The article was then treated with
a hot soldering iron, and this process
bonded or fused the silver to the tinned
surface of the piece.

The main disadvantage of close
plating was that the silver foil often
blistered and flaked off the surface.
However, this blistering is an
identifying feature and will help the
beginner distinguish between close plate
and the more expensive Sheffield Plate
(q.v.). The exposed metal is often rusty
or of a black colour.

Close plating was widely used from
about 1807 until the advent of electroplating (q.v.) in 1840. Articles usually
consisted of spoons, forks, knives, fish

slices, asparagus tongs, candle snuffers, sugar tongs (q.v.) and sugar sifting spoons. Pieces are usually marked with the maker's name or mark. These were often struck in a series of four or five punches and can be confused with silver hallmarks. The initials PS indicate 'plated steel'.

· COAL · BOXES ·
· & · SCUTTLES ·

Wood was the most common fuel in the home until the 16th century, although coal had been in use several centuries earlier, as indicated by the ban on its burning in London in 1306. An acute shortage of wood caused Elizabeth I to forbid the cutting down of some trees for converting to charcoal and burning as fuel, and so 'sea cole', so called because it was shipped down the coast from Newcastle, came into general use.

By the end of the 18th century, the humble wooden, brass-bound bucket had been replaced by a variety of coal containers. The tall, straight-sided hod with its carrying and lifting handles was made in brass, as were the round-bellied helmet scuttles, although these were also produced in steel. Pretty square boxes in japanned metal were set on wheels for ease of movement, and small boxes were produced for bedroom use.

Two pine purdoniums with brass fittings; £45–£50.

Victorian copper coal
scuttle; £90–£120.

The Victorians also favoured boxes
which had a drop-down sloping front.
These were originally made in black
enamelled tinplate with decorative brass
hinges and detachable liners, and were
the invention of a Mr Purdon who first
showed his 'purdoniums' at the Great
Exhibition in 1851. Later boxes were
made in brass, and in wood with brass or
copper decoration. Some purdoniums
had a small wooden-handled brass
shovel which slotted neatly into a looped
bar at the back of the box. Brass
purdoniums had attractively embossed
lids and the patterns were often
classical, with urns and swagged
garlands being popular. The purdonium
was also made in a larger size,
resembling a pot cupboard, the 'door' of
which swung downwards to expose the
contents.

The Edwardians had a great choice of
coal containers and a catalogue for 1907
shows them as attractively bucket-
shaped (the Wellington, and the
Waterloo), as a cauldron (the Gypsy),
and as lidded boxes, both round or
square, as well as the traditional styles.
Materials used were brass, antique or
polished copper, black japanned metal,
or galvanised zinc.

Coal scuttles are still a popular item
in the home, and Victorian and
Georgian designs are much reproduced.

19th-century tin coal
scuttle; £25–£30.

When buying, it is important to recognise the difference. Old brass is generally paler in tone than modern brass, and the brass is thicker and heavier than modern sheet brass.

It is important to check the condition of a scuttle as the base is frequently worn thin and can be holed. Liners for purdoniums are often in a poor condition, but unless the box is intended for use, damage to these liners is acceptable. If a coal shovel is present, check that the scooping edge is not split or worn, and that the handle is secure.

Victorian brass or copper scuttles will cost about £70–£80 upwards; a small purdonium in wood and brass will be about £60–£100, while an attractive cupboard-style example will be about the same price.

· COFFEE · MILLS · · & · GRINDERS ·

Although coffee had been drunk in Europe since the 17th and 18th centuries, when coffee houses flourished, it was not ground in the home until the mid-19th century. Previous to that, the customer would buy his coffee beans and have them ground by the retailer who would have a large cast iron mill.

The first domestic coffee grinder consisted of a square box with a turning handle on top which operated the grinder. The ground coffee would fall into a small drawer below. Later grinders were made of brass and iron in similar style.

A table model was introduced at the turn of the century. This was clamped to the table and rather resembled a mincer. The beans were fed into an enamelled hopper to be milled and the ground coffee then fell into a small

Early wooden coffee grinder dating from c.1810; £300.

integral dish.

Victorian coffee grinders of about 1850, made in walnut or pine, will be about £50–£60, while a later model, also made in wood, will cost about £15–£20.

· CORKSCREWS ·

Up until the end of the 17th century, bottles or flasks had been sealed with bungs of plaster or wood, loose-fitting conical corks, or else the wine was drawn straight from the cask. When it was discovered that wine improved by being kept in a bottle which was tightly corked, it was realised that a custom-made implement was needed for pulling the cork. A simple worm screw had been in use since Tudor times and wine augers and broaching gimlets were to hand for attending to the bungs and spigots on casks.

The basic principle has changed very little over the years, with the corkscrew consisting of a spiral helix or worm, made in steel and fluted for added strength, and a shaft which was fitted with a grip or handle. This could be made of silver, bronzed steel, brass, iron, horn, mother-of-pearl, ivory, bone, wood, or could be leather covered.

Eighteenth-century corkscrews were

Wooden coffee grinder with drawer below; £15–£25.

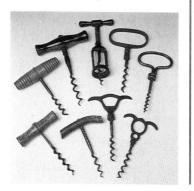

Selection of corkscrews in metal, some with wooden or bone handles; £8–£12.

simply made with a short worm and a circular or ovoid handle, but by the end of the century, they had evolved into the well-known T-bar shape. Sometimes, the wooden grips were barrel shaped and fitted with a dusting brush made from hog bristle. This enabled the neck of the bottle to be brushed free of the broken sealing wax that had protected the cork.

Variations on this simple shape included metal bow screws, which had the handle transformed into an oval ring of metal. Eyebrow screws had two wings of metal sprouting from either side of the oval handle. A simplification of this had the two wings springing from the shaft, without a ring. Travelling folding screws had an open triangular handle into which the screw fitted. These sometimes had a buttonhook and/or other implements alongside the screw. (See BUTTONHOOKS & SHOEHORNS.) A champagne corkscrew had a spiked handle for breaking the wire that held the cork, and the helix was based on the Archimedean screw. A travelling corkscrew, known as a peg and worm screw, had a detachable sheath which slotted into a hole at the top of the shaft to be used as a handle. Small wire corkscrews were sold with medicine bottles. By the 19th century, over 400 different designs had been patented.

Early in the 19th century, the first mechanical corkscrew made its appearance. Thomason's Patent was a

The 'London Lever' which was used in conjunction with a corkscrew. Once the screw had been inserted into the cork, the Lever was slipped over the neck of the bottle and, when the handles were squeezed together, the hooked part caught the corkscrew and levered it and the cork out of the bottle (Hastings Museum).

hermaphroditic corkscrew which had both male and female threads. The screw was inserted into the cork and turned clockwise for secure insertion. The counter-threaded screw ensured that the cork was gradually drawn out of the bottle by carrying on this clockwise motion. The King's Screw was made in around 1830 and was based on the rack and pinion principle, as was the 'London Rack' made by Lund. The A1 Double Lever, patented by Heeley & Son, was based on a series of linked levers, rather like the 'lazy tongs' principle.

Corkscrew with silver-mounted horn handle and square spike.

There is very little to check when buying corkscrews, other than to ensure that the worm is not bent or broken at the tip. The workings on mechanical screws might be subject to wear but this is acceptable, providing there is no significant damage.

Corkscrews vary enormously in price, from £3 to £10 for a plain steel corkscrew with an oval ring or eyebrow handle, to between £70–£250 for a King's Screw. Any pre-Victorian corkscrew will cost around £200, although rare examples can be even more. A bone-handled corkscrew with dusting brush will be about £65–£75; one with a turned wooden handle costs about £25–£35 and one with a plain wooden handle will be about £10–£20.

· CRADLES · & · · COTS ·

At the end of the 18th century, rocking cradles were generally of two types: those that were suspended on wooden supports and could be moved gently to and fro, and cribs that were floor standing, on curved rockers.

A magnificent swinging cradle was made for Queen Victoria's first child in

1843. It was boat shaped with the open mahogany ribs being padded with green satin. The arched mahogany stand which held the cradle was carved, and decorated with gold leaf and brass mounts. Swags of matching satin were draped on the frame and protected the child from any draught.

Floor-standing cradles or cribs could be made entirely of wood with solid sides and an overhanging hood and decorated in the Jacobean style, or could be in the Gothic style, with an arched hood, and constructed with lightweight panels of canework set between walnut or mahogany supports. Smaller wicker cribs were of a more open construction with only a suggestion of a hood and with quilted, padded sides. These came with or without rockers.

Cots were generally larger than cradles and were intended for older infants. They stood on legs rather than being suspended or having rockers, and had high, straight sides. These could be made of wood with railed sides, have panels of canework, or could be of open wicker construction.

Metal cots and cradles became fashionable at the turn of the century. High-sided cots were made in cast iron and these could stand on castors. Portable, collapsible cots, called bassinets, were made with frames of

Early wooden cradle set on rockers. Length 39 inches (99 cm), width 18 inches (45.7 cm), height 28 inches (71 cm); £250–£300.

Folding bassinet, made in metal and string. Length 38 inches (96.5 cm), width 18 inches (45.5 cm), height 36 inches (91.5 cm); £100–£125.

iron or brass. The cots were available in white or japanned black, and were designed to be trimmed. Frilled flounces could be bought to cover the sides of the cot and these were made in muslin or lace with wide satin ribbon bows. A tall hooked tube of metal was fixed to the back of the cot as an end-piece and 'curtains' of muslin and lace were arranged artistically over this to fall either side of the head of the cot.

Victorian cradles were often based on older styles and care should be taken when buying. A Jacobean cradle is considerably rarer than its Victorian copy and worth far more. Carving on later cradles is usually shallow and will show signs of being machine-cut rather than hand-carved. The swinging mechanism should be checked as this was subject to much usage and may show signs of wear. Cane and wickerwork should be checked for holes and splits.

Cots and cradles are not cheap to buy. A Victorian reproduction of the Gothic style, made in canework and in good condition, will cost £250–£500. A wickerwork cot will cost about £100–£250, as will a large cast iron cot with high, straight sides. Edwardian bassinets will cost between about £50–£150.

· CRUMB ·
· SCOOPS ·
TRAYS & BRUSHES

These useful domestic implements came into fashion around the mid-1900s and stayed popular through to about 1940–50. The fastidious housewife would have them to hand for clearing the table after high tea. Rather than shaking out the tablecloth, any crumbs would be scooped up and deposited into the oval waiter, or swept neatly into the matching tray.

The scoop was a flat oblong of metal, sometimes slightly curved, and with one straight edge. Handles would be of turned wood, ivory, bone or mother-of-pearl. The crumbs were prevented from falling off the scoop by a shallow raised strip of metal. The scoop was used without a brush, the straight edge making short work of scraping up the crumbs.

The brush was curved with short bristles, and was used in conjunction with a tray shaped rather like a dustpan. This could be ornately embossed if made of silver, silver-plate, EPNS (electro-plated nickel silver), brass or copper. Chromium-plated metal sets and those made of wood such as oak and mahogany were generally of a plain style.

Crumb trays and brushes are

TOP: Wooden tray and brush set; £10–£15.
BOTTOM: Painted crumb brush; £5–£8.

Copper crumb tray and brush with Art Nouveau pattern pressed in relief; £15–£25.

frequently separated from each other
and mismatched sets made up. Care
should be taken, when buying, that one
matches the other. As the leading edge
on a crumb scoop was frequently of
extreme thinness, it was prone to wear
and splits, and so should be examined
carefully.

Prices are still fairly low. A set of
brush and tray made in wood will cost
from about £10–£15, one in silver-plate
of ornate embossed design will cost
£50–£70 upwards. A crumb scoop in
brass with a turned ebonised handle will
be about £10–£20; one in silver-plate
with a mother-of-pearl handle will be
about £35–£50 upwards.

· CUT-THROAT ·
· RAZORS ·

The first razor is thought to have been
used by the Romans in about 454 BC,
and men have veered between being
bearded or not ever since. In the 1880s,
it was the fashion to be clean-shaven
and gentlemen either employed the
services of a barber, shaved themselves
or relied on their valet to do it for them.

The most vital piece of equipment
was a finely honed razor. This would
have a long, slightly curved blade which,
when not in use, folded over and fitted
neatly into its handle. This type of
shaving implement had been used since
the 1600s but the use of steel in the
manufacture meant that the Victorian
razor was a superior instrument. The
curved blade was sharpened daily by
grinding with a slate or carborundum
block, or by honing it against a leather
strop.

The appeal of cut-throat razors lies in
their handles. Although basically of the
same shape and style, they were made
in a variety of materials. Ivory, bone,

'Puma' razor with
matching Bakelite case;
£15–£20.

C

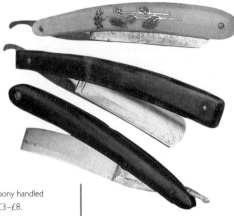

TOP: Ebony handled razor; £3–£8.
CENTRE: Razor with tortoiseshell handle; £10–£15.
BOTTOM: Ivory handled razor, set with enamelled flowers outlined in silver; £15–£20.

Boxed honing stone and razor with ivorine handle; £5–£10.

horn and tortoiseshell are perhaps the most common, and plastics such as Bakelite, ivorine and celluloid. Some razors were decorated with silver mounting on the handles and tortoiseshell guards on the blades, or the handles could be set with inlaid enamels. Razors can also be found with the handles made of ornately carved mother-of-pearl.

Pairs of razors were intended to be used on alternate days and these can be found attractively boxed. Sets of seven razors, one for each day of the week, were also boxed and were individually numbered or marked 'Sunday', 'Monday' and so on.

Cut-throat razors of the plainer variety can still be found fairly cheaply. One with a black Bakelite handle will cost about £3–£15 while those with tortoiseshell handles are about £10–£30. Enamelled examples are between £20–£60. An early 19th-century boxed pair with tortoiseshell handles and ornate silver mounts will be about £150–£180, while a boxed set of seven razors will be from £50–£70 upwards, depending on the handles.

d

· DOOR ·
· FURNITURE ·

Door knockers fall into two types: those
with a solid pendant-style rapper or
hammer that was lifted and knocked
against the door itself or against a plain
or ornamental back plate, and those
with a ring or oval of metal that relied
on a decorative back plate for appeal.
Perhaps the most often seen of the
latter is the cast iron lion's head with a
ring suspended from its mouth.

The solid rappers were based on
classical designs such as the urn, or a
grasping hand which held a baton or bar
against a background of a laurel wreath
or fruiting vine. The ring-type rapper
incorporated both animal and mask-like
human heads, often grotesque in design.
A great many knockers were produced
at Coalbrookdale, the centre of the cast
iron industry, and those bearing the
diamond-shaped registry mark (see
REGISTERED DESIGN MARKS) are sought
after.

Brass knockers had been made since
the late 17th century, but they increased
in popularity in the early 19th century
with the development of new brass
alloys which were stronger and more
able to stand up to the hard knocking.
These too used animals and heads as a
theme, with goats, lions, serpents,
dolphins and even the mask of Medusa
being made.

With the introduction of the penny
post in 1840, door knockers began to
include a small letter box, and these
gradually evolved into separate items of
door furniture. Some were intended
solely for the insertion of the mail,
others had a handle-shaped rapper built
into the design, so doing away with the
traditional door knocker. Cast iron
examples can have the word 'Letters'

Heavy curved Regency
door knocker in brass.
Length 10 inches
(25.4 cm).

moulded into them, but perhaps more popular are those made in shining brass.

Finger plates were used on interior doors to protect the door from unsightly marks. These were made in brass, steel, and porcelain, with the 1920s seeing them made in perspex, Bakelite, pressed brass or tin.

Porcelain finger plates were usually decorated with sprays of flowers, while brass plates could be reeded, embossed with cherubs or classical garlands and wreaths, or could be cast in an ornate filigree pattern. The finger plates were often part of a matching set of door knobs or handles, and key plates or escutcheons.

Door knobs and handles are also collectable. Handles usually consisted of an upright elongated back plate on to which the baton-style handle was fixed. The back plate could be of embossed brass, with a brass-mounted porcelain or glass handle. Knobs were made in brass, cut glass, porcelain or china, and polished wood.

There is a great deal of reproduction door furniture on sale at present and great care must be taken when buying. A reputable dealer will ensure that reproduction goods are sold as such, and will advise regarding the age of antique door furniture. Avoid any pieces that are bright and 'brassy'; old brass mellows

Mid-19th-century lion's head knocker with a rope-design ring and a smaller head as the rapper.

LEFT: Two brass door knockers; £15–£25.
RIGHT: Two door knockers made in cast iron; £15–£25.

d

Finger plates in wood, pottery, brass, and black terracotta; £5–£15.

with age. Letter boxes should be checked for wear, the hinge that closes the flap is often weak and ineffectual with constant use. Tarnished brass responds well to cleaning with a proprietary cleaner, although this may take a great deal of hard work if there is much embossing or ornamentation.

Prices for early door knockers will start at about £20–£30 for one in plain style; an animal's head knocker will cost about £50–£60. Letter boxes can be found quite cheaply. A cast iron example with 'Letters' embossed will be about £10–£15; a plain brass letter box will be about £15 upwards. Finger plates are also relatively inexpensive, and a pressed brass plate with an embossed pattern will be about £10–£15 upwards. Brass door knobs will be about £5–£10; those in cut glass cost about £15–£20, but these should be carefully checked for chips.

· DOOR · STOPS ·

In the late 18th century, John Izon and Thomas Whitehurst invented and patented rising butt hinges. This meant that doors closed automatically, so eliminating draughts. However, some

d

doors were better left open, and so the door stop or door porter came into being.

These were made in heavy cast iron, although they can also be found in brass and lead, and were round, rather than the later flatter shape. Lions were shown standing with a paw resting on a large ball, or could be found lying down or *en couchant* and looking rather more like docile dogs. Bell-shaped door stops had a ring-like handle for ease of lifting.

With the development of casting techniques, door stops in iron were mass-produced. Perhaps the most popular design was that of Mr Punch, sometimes seen as a pair with his wife, Judy. Animals, too, were favoured and one can find stags and lions, cats, dogs, horses, foxes, deer and elephants, and birds such as the swan or eagle. Sphinx heads, dolphins and lions' paws were also favoured. Notable people of the day were featured and Wellington, Nelson, Gladstone, Disraeli, Prince Albert and Queen Victoria were all immortalised in cast iron.

In the early 19th century, it was fashionable to have painted door stops. These were made with an 'artistic bronze' finish, or decorated in bright primary colours. Later door stops were left unpainted, being polished with blacking to give them a gloss.

Some reproduction door stops are being made today, particularly Punch and Judy, so when buying, check the quality of the casting. If the cast iron is dull and grey-looking, an application of grate cleaner or boot blacking followed by vigorous buffing will soon restore the brightness.

Prices start at about £30 for those in both brass and cast iron, about £60–£70 upwards for those depicting well-known personalities.

· EGG · OPENERS ·

In the mid-1900s, a device was patented which guaranteed to 'facilitate the removal of the ends of eggs'. There were several names for this useful implement: egg openers, cutters, toppers, shears, biters and slicers, and during the years that followed, the Victorians, ever inventive, came up with an astonishing variety. These varied between a device that guided the knife accurately for 'slitting' the egg, to one with a scissor-like action that dealt with the egg effectively.

The opener which guided the knife consisted of a handled ring of metal or china which sat over the end of the egg. The knife was then slid firmly across the exposed surface, topping the egg neatly.

The scissor type had a ring of metal instead of one blade and a flat slicing disc instead of the other. When the looped handles were brought together sharply, the 'blades' would snap closed, so decapitating the egg. The shafts between the handles and the business ends of the openers were often stamped out in the form of a hen or cockerel, and a catalogue for 1907 shows that this type of 'egg cutter' was obtainable for one shilling (five pence).

Early egg openers were made in silver, silver-plate, plated nickel, or base metal. Modern egg openers are still being made, but these are generally chromed or made in stainless steel. Designs have changed very little over the years, and care must be taken when buying, although older hens and cockerels are generally cast in more detail than modern examples. A specialist dealer will be helpful.

Prices will start at about £5 or £6; more if the opener has cockerel shafts.

· ELECTRO- ·
· PLATING ·

Between about 1836 and 1840, George
Richards Elkington and his cousin
Henry Elkington separately patented
three methods of electroplating base
metal. This replaced Sheffield Plate
(q.v.), and enabled articles made in
silver to be copied quickly and cheaply.

Electroplating was a method of
covering one metal (usually copper
alloys of tin, zinc or nickel) with a thin
deposit or layer of another by means of
electrolytic action. The object to be
plated was suspended in a bath of
electrolytic solution, while at the
opposite pole or anode, a piece of the
plating metal was immersed. When an
electric charge was passed between the
two, particles of the plating metal
detached themselves from the plating
piece and adhered to the surface of the
item that was to be plated. The method
was used on finished articles and
enabled goods to be mass-produced
from die-stamped copper sheets.

The Elkington process used gold
(electro-gilding) and silver for plating,
while a method patented by Joseph
Shore in 1840 used copper and nickel
for electroplating. Later plating came to
be known as EPNS (electroplated
nickel silver).

When buying plated articles, ensure
that the plating is not scratched or worn.
If it has a yellow tinge then the nickel
base is showing through, and the piece
should be avoided unless it is decorative
and desirable. Re-plating can be done
but this will tend to devalue the piece.

(See also SHEFFIELD PLATE.)

Silver-plated match or
vesta case.

· E · P · N · S ·
See Electro-Plating

·FENDERS·

Up until the late 18th century, fireplaces were built with large wide hearths of stone or marble, and so there was no need for a fender to protect the carpet from burning logs or coals that might fall from the grate. However, with the fashion for raised cast iron grates, promoted by the classical designs of the Adams brothers, fenders became necessary. There was a shortage of brass at the time, so the brothers imported paktong, an alloy with a high zinc content capable of withstanding fierce heat. The alloy was hard and durable and its silver colour remained free from tarnish.

As the manufacture of fenders became established, other metals were used, including brass, gunmetal, bell metal, cut steel, copper, and later, in the early 19th century, cast iron. Matching sets of fire irons (q.v.) were also made in brass or steel.

Early fenders were simply a strip of metal of curved or serpentine shape, and without side supports. Designs were classical, often matching the fire grate, and the fenders were pierced or fretted decoratively, some having additional ornamental bosses. After about 1800, fenders became square ended, with

TOP: Cast-iron fender. Length 40 inches (101 cm); £60.
BOTTOM: Cast-iron fender. Length 20 inches (51 cm); £33.

supporting side pieces for greater stability. A cast iron or tinplate 'apron' was sometimes riveted to the fender to give protection from sparks and falling embers.

Fenders could be heavily fretted in lattice patterns, or could have embossed designs or applied decoration. Plain brass or cast iron fenders of shallow form were sometimes surmounted by large balls set in a narrow rail, and these were generally used in the smoking, billiard or club room. Another fender popular with men was the club fender. This came complete with a padded seat end and was ideal for keeping warm in comfort on a cold winter's day. This style was popular through to the 20th century when, in the 1920s, the club fender was made in wood with barley twist rails in imitation of the Jacobean style. Another adaptation had the fender slotting into a padded box at either end, useful for storage.

Also at this time, the curb was developed. This was an abbreviated form of fender and was usually made of wood, or wood with a copper, brass or oxidised sheet metal covering.

Cast iron fenders are subject to rust, but this can be cleaned off by using a wire brush. The fender can then be polished with grate or boot blacking. Using a protective black paint with a hammer finish can make the fender look like new, but will devalue it. If

Brass fender with a pattern of large studs; £100.

buying a small copper- or brass-clad curb, ensure that the metal cladding is sound, and not split.

Prices for serpentine fenders in brass will start at about £250–£900 depending on age, complexity of pattern and design. Victorian fenders in curved steel will be about £100–£250. Square-ended fenders in brass will be from about £100–£150; those in cast iron from £50–£70 upwards. Small brass- or copper-clad curbs will be from £30 upwards; wooden club-style fenders and those dating from the 1940s in clad metal will be about £40–£60 upwards.

· FIREDOGS ·
· & · RESTS ·

The basic function of a firedog and andiron was to support the logs in a hearth so that they were subjected to the necessary draught when burning. They were simply made in cast iron at first, with bell metal and wrought iron being used later, and consisted of a horizontal bar which was supported by a pair of curved legs at either end. The supports had knopped finials which held the logs securely and prevented them from rolling off into the room. The firedogs gradually became more complex in design, and were regarded as a status symbol. Cast iron dogs were extremely elaborate, some even featuring the owner's coat of arms. Brass firedogs retained their iron supports, and were used in conjunction with humbler cast dogs, supporting only the extremities of the logs. When coal began to supersede logs as fuel, they lost their original function totally and were merely ornamental.

As the function of firedogs changed, so did their shape. The two back legs gave way to a single support. The front

LEFT: One of a pair of steel firedogs. Height 15 inches (38 cm), length 15 inches (38 cm); £52 the pair.
RIGHT: Wrought iron firedog. Height 13 inches (33 cm), length 10 inches (25.4 cm); £38 the pair.

Pair of large cast -iron firedogs. Height 18 inches (45.7 cm), length 18 inches (45.7 cm); £85 the pair.

uprights became tall balustered columns standing on two curved feet, and were finished off with imposing urn finials.

Fire rests were never meant to be used with logs, but were intended to take the fire tools that had become popular in the mid-18th century when the Adams brothers revolutionised the style of the grate. They were usually made of brass, with decorative ends, and the horizontal bar that was formerly made of iron was also of brass. They could be of a simple 'H' shape, or could have the two end supports linked by an upper and lower horizontal bar, the space being in-filled with ornate patterns of classical style.

Firedogs vary enormously in price. A pair of 18th-century dogs in wrought iron of plain design will cost about £100–£150; ornate brass examples of a slightly later period will be £500 or more. Victorian firedogs of stylish simplicity will be about £80–£150. Ornate fire rests will be about £150 upwards; those in plainer style about £50–£100.

· FIRE · SCREENS · · & · GUARDS ·

Although fire screens are reputed to have been around since the beginning of the 15th century, none have survived.

The large basket grates which threw out great heat, used in the reign of George II, made the use of fire screens almost obligatory and they became well established, although it is those from the Victorian era and later that are to be found today.

The most often seen type is the cheval screen. This was a square-shaped stand or frame which stood on bridged feet and which had a decorative panel set between two upright supports. The frame can be of brass, metal or wood, plain in style with perhaps a fretted border, or in the case of wood, barley twist supports. The panel could be of glass, enclosing an arrangement of dried flowers, or mirrored with a pattern of stylised flower heads cut into it, or with a spray of hand-painted flowers across it.

Brass fire screens were left plain, or had embossed or applied decoration. The patterns could cover the whole of the screen and be very detailed. The figure of a rearing horse was popular.

Wooden fire screens of the mid-19th century featured hand-painted pictures on silk, or gros-point needlework panels, both enclosed within glass. Later screens had panels of wool or silk

Fire screen with a bamboo frame and hand-painted flowers on a glass panel; £65.

Screen in ebonised wood with painted flower decoration; £25–£30.

Wrought iron fire screen;
£50–£60.

embroidery, also under glass, or could
be made entirely of wood with just a
little raised decoration. Small bedroom
screens, used to hide the unused
fireplace, consisted of a plain, hinged
frame on to which were fastened
pleated fabric 'curtains'.

Brass mesh screens are called
fireguards, and their purpose was to
prevent flying sparks from causing the
carpet to catch fire. These were made in
the style of fire screens and could have
applied motifs such as butterflies, or
perhaps classical emblems. Nursery
fireguards were of a large open mesh
and were not intended to catch sparks,
but to ensure the safety of infants and
small children.

Mirrored screens should be checked
for any chips to the glass. Spotting or
breaking down of the silvered back can
devalue it, but it is relatively cheap to
have a mirror re-silvered. The painting
on mirrored screens can be worn or
rubbed, and this makes the piece
unattractive. Wooden screens should be
checked for woodworm, and mesh
screens should be examined for splits or
tears. Handles and feet should be firm
and sound and not wobbly or loose.

Brass fire screens are easily found and

cost from about £30–£50 upwards.
Painted mirrored screens are from about
£30–£60, but much depends on the
quality of the painting. Embroidered
20th-century screens are from about
£30, and plain wooden screens cost
about £10–£20. Mesh fireguards of
small size will be about £20–£40
upwards; large sizes from £40–£80.

· FIRE · TOOLS ·

Tools for use in the hearth became
popular with the introduction of the
smaller grate in the mid-18th century.
They were made in brass, wrought iron,
steel, or brass combined with steel or
iron, and came in sets which comprised
a poker, tongs and a shovel. The shovel
was originally bell-shaped with lightly
raised and curved sides, and was pierced
and fretted decoratively. This piercing
allowed the ashes to be effectively sifted
from the embers. By the end of the
18th century, the bell shape had given
way to a more rectangular form and
embossing was added to piercing and
fretting as decoration, or used alone.
Both shovel and poker had long, hollow-
core-cast handles which could be fluted

Shovel with pierced pan
and a selection of pokers.
Shovel £10–£20; pokers
£5–£10.

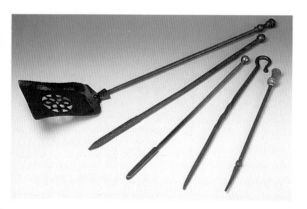

Selection of fire tongs in iron, brass, and iron with a brass finial; £20–£25.

or attractively knopped, and these could measure as much as 4 feet (1.22 m) in length overall but were more usually about 2 feet (60 cm) long. The tongs were equally long, finishing in flat disc-like ends when used for wood, claw-ended for coal.

The fire tools were set on fire rests (see FIREDOGS) which had been adapted from the firedog, and it was not until the 1920s that a purpose-built stand appeared. Known as a companion set, it was sold complete with a set of hanging tools comprising a poker, shovel, tongs and a hearth brush. The stand and tools were made in brass, oxidised metal and chromium-plated metal.

When buying fire irons, check the handles on the shovels. Although these were often riveted, they did break due to stress and usage. Rewelding will shorten them, so the length should be checked. The scooping edge should also be checked for splits and excessive usage. The hinges on tongs also show signs of wear, which means that the tongs flop about and are useless for all practical purposes. The threading on brass-covered iron rods can be worn, making the tool unusable. The decorative hanging tops on companion sets should match correctly, and the brush should not be burnt or worn.

Prices for very early fire tools in polished steel are very high and a set can cost as much as £1500. Later Victorian and Edwardian tools are more affordable at about £70–£100 upwards. Companion sets from the 1920s are about £30–£60 for brass; about £15 upwards for chromium plate.

· FLAT · IRONS ·

See Irons

· GRAMOPHONES ·

The first phonograph was produced by Thomas Alva Edison in 1877. It consisted of a needle or stylus which was set in a diaphragm attached to a mouthpiece. The stylus scratched the surface of a rotating cylinder that was wrapped in tinfoil. The principle worked well enough, but the machine was cumbersome and the foil soon wore out. In 1888, Edison replaced the foil-wrapped cylinder with one of solid wax. A year or two before that, Alexander Graham Bell, together with his cousin Chichester Bell, and an instrument maker called Charles Tainter, had experimented with a wax-covered cardboard cylinder. They called their machine a graphophone, and considered it ideal for taking dictation in the office.

The phonograph continued in popularity well into the 20th century, being manufactured until about 1929. In 1912, a more robust cylinder was made, having a plaster-of-Paris centre and a plastic coating; it was played with a diamond stylus.

As cylinders developed and became more sophisticated, so they varied in size and in 1899, Edison's 'Concert Phonograph' was equipped with a large cylinder 5 inches (12.7 cm) in diameter. In 1908, a four-minute cylinder was

Edison 'Fireside' phonograph (minus the horn) c.1906.

g

The 'Direct-O-Phone'
gramophone c.1910 with
large green painted horn;
£350–£400.

marketed; this had 200 grooves to the
inch instead of the former 100. In the
late 1800s, a German immigrant living
in Washington DC, Emile Berliner,
invented the gramophone which used
wax-coated zinc discs instead of
cylinders. As these discs were capable of
being press moulded, thousands of
copies could be made from the master
disc, unlike the waxed cylinder which
had to be painstakingly copied a few at a
time. Discs were made in vulcanised
rubber, but these were unsuccessful as
reproduction was poor, and they were
soon replaced by records made of
shellac. In 1897, the one-sided discs
were 5 and 7 inches (12.7 cm and 17.7
cm) in diameter; in 1901, the 10-inch
(25.4 cm) disc appeared, and in 1903
the familiar 12-inch (30.5 cm) record
arrived.

The horn had, by now, been
extended to a huge size with some
almost 6 feet (1.8 m) in length. They
were made in polished brass,
aluminium, painted tinplate, papier-
mâché and wood, such as mahogany.
The horn could either be of a straight

conical shape, or flared in a witch's-hat style. The latter later evolved into the 'flower' or 'Morning Glory' shape that was made from pressed sheet metal, or assembled in 'petals'. HMV (His Master's Voice) gramophones featured 'Nipper' the dog as their trademark and he was sometimes cast in plaster to sit by the side of the machine.

In 1904 the German Hymnophone was produced, and this had the horn enclosed in the casing. It made the gramophone more portable, and the first of these portables was issued during the First World War. Known as the 'Celeste' or 'Trench', the gramophone was widely used in the trenches. By the 1920s, the exterior horn had virtually disappeared, although a few companies were still making them throughout the 1930s, with the HMV 102 portable being available in 1960.

Early horned gramophones are expensive and one with a 'witch's hat' horn in brass dating from about 1900 will be over £1000, as will be an early phonograph of similar style. A gramophone with a brass flower horn will cost about £500–£600, while a mahogany-horned example will be about £700–£800. A mahogany table gramophone with concealed speakers dating from the 1930s will be between £150–£200. An HMV portable with black leather covering will be about £50, while those with green, blue or red Leatherette coverings will be dearer, with prices starting at around £100–£250.

HMV (His Master's Voice) gramophone in a collectable blue case; £150–£200.

· GRATERS ·

Various graters and rasps have been designed to cope with different tasks in the kitchen. The wooden-handled bread rasp consisted of a strip of metal, usually

g

Group of graters between
5 inches (12.7 cm) and
8 inches (20.3 cm);
50p–£2.

iron, which had a roughened surface.
This was used for scraping any burnt
part off the loaf, and also for grating
stale bread into breadcrumbs.

Cheese and vegetable graters were
made of tinplate and consisted of a flat
section of metal with raised piercing.
Alternatively, they could be made with
a flat back and curved front. Early 20th-
century graters were made in round,
tubular form or were three-sided in
triangular fashion. The latter often had
holes of varying size for multiple use.

A larger and more sophisticated grater
was incorporated horizontally into a
wooden frame. The grated food then
fell through the holes to the drawer
below.

Tiny graters were used for spices and
these were often made in pairs and kept
boxed in a tin.

Tin graters can be found for about
£3–£5 each, more cheaply at car boot
sales or jumble sales. Bread rasps cost
about £10–£20. A pair of spice graters
complete with their tin will be £20–£30
or more, while large wooden-framed
graters will be £50-plus.

(See also NUTMEG GRATERS.)

h

·HALLMARKS·

In 1478 a system of hallmarking was
devised which gave an indication of the
standard of gold and silver articles. An
assay mark, town mark and date letter
were stamped on to the metal, and
occasionally the maker's mark was also
included.

It was intended that the hallmarks
should run in 20-year cycles and these
were differentiated by varying the style
of the shield which enclosed the various
marks. The date letters were also varied
by using a different style of lettering, for
example, Gothic or italic script.

The principal assay offices where the
metal was tested were London,
Birmingham and Sheffield, and the
marks for these were a leopard's head,
an anchor and a crown, respectively.
There were also assay offices at Chester,
Dublin, Edinburgh, Exeter, Glasgow
and York.

The standard for gold is calculated in
carats, each carat being a twenty-fourth
part. This gives a guide to the purity of
the gold; an alloy having 22 parts of
gold to 24 parts of the whole is classified
as 22 carat gold. Pure gold is never used
as it is too soft. The standard mark is
sometimes shown as 916 (22 carat), 750
(18 carat), 585 (14 carat) and 375 (9
carat). Imported gold carries the same
standard marks as those for British gold.

Silver consisting of 958 parts per
thousand is known as Britannia silver,
and if it consists of 925 parts per
thousand it is called Sterling silver.

·HERB·
·CHOPPERS·

Used for chopping basil, marjoram,
rosemary, parsley and thyme, as well as
for various vegetables, the herb chopper

Herb choppers; £10–£15.

often resembled a small spade with a curved blade that was minus its shaft. Early choppers were often very decorative with pierced blades and attractively carved fruitwood handles, but with the advent of mechanisation in the Industrial Revolution, choppers were mass-produced in plain styles.

The turned wooden handle was usually T-shaped and firmly riveted on to the rectangular iron blade. When the blade was curved, the chopper was intended to be used in conjunction with a wooden bowl. A curved blade would sometimes have two handles, one at either end, and this was used in a rocking motion.

Herb choppers are readily found, but the handles should be examined when buying. These will sometimes have been replaced, and will be screwed on rather than riveted. Avoid choppers where the blade is badly pitted.

Prices start at about £10–£12 for a plain, mass-produced example, but if the curved chopper is complete with its wooden bowl then it will cost between £50–£100.

· HOT · WATER ·
· BOTTLES ·

Up until the end of the 18th century, beds had been heated by the use of hot coals placed in warming pans (q.v.). The introduction of boiling water as a heating element did away with the risk of fire. The traditional frying pan shape was retained, as was the long handle, but the pan was made watertight by means of a screw stopper set at the top or side. By the beginning of the 19th century, the handle had been largely dispensed with, and a cylindrical shape had become an alternative to the round flat-bottomed container.

Earthenware hot water bottles gradually replaced the metal warmers and these were affectionately known as 'pigs'. They were of a cylindrical shape with a flattened bottom, rather like a log, with a screw-top opening at the top or at one end.

Early examples were decorated with blue and white tin glazing, or had a 'scratched' decoration incised into them. Victorian bottles were of whitestone and this could be two-tone or decorated with transfer-printed designs.

The stone hot water bottle retained its popularity up until the late 1930s.

Selection of earthenware hot water bottles; £10–£15.

Grimwades 'Winton' pottery 'Mecca Footwarmer' with transfer-printed design. Height 11 inches (28 cm); £150.

Some were most attractive; Grimwades, for example, decorated theirs with transfer-printed roses, while Langley made one in a pot-bellied shape in two-tone honey glaze, and it came complete with a leather carrying handle. A bottle resembling a Gladstone bag had the initials B.E.D. stamped on the side. Doulton made humorous bottles in the shapes of bears and dogs. In the 1920s, Denby produced a shouldered bottle called 'The Bungalow Footwarmer'. This bore a black and white picture of a bungalow, together with the company name. Retailers also had them made to their own design, and bottles such as the 'Reliable' hot water bottle and bed warmer could be bought from the chemists, Timothy White.

The first moulded rubber hot water bottle appeared as early as the 1890s and gradually superseded the earthenware 'pig'. These were pillow shaped with a carrying handle and a screw top, a design which has hardly changed over the years. A retailer's catalogue for 1907 shows rubber hot water bottles designed for different parts of the body. An elongated version was intended to be wrapped around the throat; an oblong bottle came in two sizes, one for the chest, a larger model for the back. Tiny bottles were made especially for placing on the ear or the eye, while a flat, triangular bottle was ideal for stomach ache.

Plain 20th-century earthenware hot water bottles can be found at auction for under £10, but more attractive examples are harder to find. A two-tone Langley bottle will be about £20–£50, with a transfer-printed 'advertising' bottle costing about the same, depending on the design. A hot water bottle with floral decoration will be between £50–£100, as will a Gladstone bag bottle.

Trademark seen on the base of the 'Mecca Footwarmer'.

·INKSTANDS·

Originally called a standish, the inkstand was made in silver, Sheffield plate, wood and porcelain. It usually consisted of a casket or shallow tray fitted with ink pots, and space for pens (see PENS AND PENCILS), taper sticks, seals, sealing wax, and pounce pots. The latter held the sand, pounded pumice or resin that was sprinkled on to the document to dry the ink and stop it from spreading across the page.

Later 19th-century inkstands were less formal in design and consisted of the tray or base which sometimes had a carrying handle, and was equipped with bottles for both red and black ink, a pen holder or rack, and a small lidded box or drawer for stamps and/or pen nibs.

Victorian inkstands were made in polished wood, sometimes ebonised, brass, bronze and porcelain. Simple wooden trays with just an indentation for the pen would have pierced brass holders to contain the ink pots, or they would have ornamental glass bottles that fitted into cut-out indentations on the tray. These occasionally came with a small drawer fitted with a brass handle.

Painted wooden inkstand; £25–£30.

Pressed glass stands were equally simple, consisting merely of an indented tray, complete with two ink pots. These were later copied in Bakelite.

When buying, the ink pots should be checked for damage, and also that they match the inkstand in age. They are frequently replaced. Glass ink pots should be checked for chips and cracks, and a good fit to the lid. Hinges on brass or silver-plated capped pots should also be examined for wear.

Prices will vary enormously. Early porcelain inkstands will be over £200, decorative bronze about £400-plus, while silver examples will cost more

i

Silver hallmarked inkstand, presented to Miss M. Bethan Edwards in August 1907.

then £1000. More affordable are the wooden trays with a shallow drawer, and these are about £50–£100. Brass stands will be about £25–£50, depending on how ornate the design is. Pressed glass and Bakelite inkstands will start at about £15–£20, although a 1930s Bakelite example trimmed with chrome and glass will be about £25–£50.

· INKWELLS ·

These were used independently of the inkstand (q.v.) and were often extremely decorative or novel in appearance. They were made in a wide variety of designs in metal, pottery, porcelain and glass. Porcelain containers were often set on an integral round tray that was used to hold the pen or for catching drips, and were decorated with delicate hand-painted flowers. Novelty shapes introduced in the late 19th and 20th centuries included clowns, faces, owls, greyhounds and other animals. Inkwells could also be of a plain, square shape with a bulbous cap set on a brass hinge.

Metal inkwells complete with ceramic liners were made in pewter, brass, silver plate and cast iron, and were often of 'capstan' design.

With the introduction of mechanisation, pressed glass inkwells

Glass inkwell with ceramic dipper/cap.

were made in great numbers. These could be of round or square cushion shape with either matching glass lids, or caps of brass, copper or silver plate. Some were made in pink Cranberry glass and placed in openwork copper 'cages' with matching metal caps. Souvenir inkwells were set on small oval or boat-shaped stands and featured a sepia photograph of the holiday resort fixed in a glass medallion.

Travelling inkwells were popular during the late 18th and 19th centuries. These consisted of a leather-covered round or square box containing the glass pot. This was covered by a brass lid which was fitted with an ingenious spring mechanism to ensure a tight fit and no leakage.

Square-shape, hand-painted porcelain inkwells will cost about £30–£50; a similar shape in cut glass will be about £25–£40. A Cranberry glass inkwell made at the turn of the century, and with decorative copper casing, will be £30–£60. An Art Deco inkwell in the shape of a clown will be £100–£150.

Travelling inkwells vary in size and price. The smallest will be £10–£20, while one of round shape will cost about £15–£25. Larger square 'box' varieties will be about £40–£60. Glass souvenir inkwells cost from about £15–£20, while simple glass containers with matching lids and possibly separated from their original inkstands can be found from about £5–£10.

LEFT: Brass-capped inkwell c.1860;
CENTRE TOP: glass inkwell c.1870.
RIGHT: souvenir inkwell containing sand from Alum Bay in the Isle of Wight c.1890. All £10–£15.
CENTRE BOTTOM: inkwell marking the Great Exhibition of 1851; £45.

irons

Although the Romans are known to have used wooden presses in laundering, it is the Chinese who are credited with the use of the first smoothing tool. As early as the 8th century, they were using saucepan-like smoothers to press the creases out of their clothes. In the 9th century, the Vikings used a mushroom-shaped stone and this gradually evolved into the 'slicker', a black glass ball that was rubbed over the creases.

The first reference to the use of heated flat irons in Europe occurs in the 17th century but it was not until the following century that the first patent was taken out when Isaac Wilkinson designed a heated box iron.

The box iron was made of iron and had a hollow interior. An iron slug would be heated until red hot, then lifted with tongs and slipped into the opening. A hinged or sliding lid or door at the heel or top of the iron kept the slug safely in place. A spare slug would be heating while the iron was being used. The box iron was sharply pointed and was ideal for the many gathers used in costume at that time.

Charcoal iron made by T & C Clark & Co. Patented 21 May 1867 (Hastings Museum).

Box iron complete with inner slug and hinged back plate (Hastings Museum).

The box iron was gradually superseded by the charcoal or ember iron. This was heated by means of burning charcoal or hot embers and a series of holes were punched in the sides of the iron to let out the fumes; alternatively, the iron was fitted with a funnel or chimney-like spout. The holes were arranged decoratively and were triangular, scroll or clover-shaped. More sophisticated irons had a small opening that could be opened or closed to create a draught, thus regulating the temperature.

'Sad' irons were of solid construction (the name being a corruption of the word 'solid') with a tempered steel face and hollow handle. They were heated by standing on end near a special stove, or close to the glowing coals of a fire. They were designed to be used in pairs, with one heating while the other was in use. Disadvantages were the frequent sooting of the steel face, and scorching caused by overheating of the iron. Despite these disadvantages, the sad iron increased in popularity until by the late 19th century they were in general use, and continued to be made until the mid-1930s.

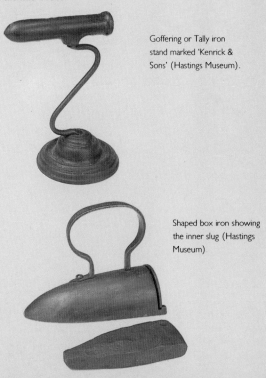

Goffering or Tally iron stand marked 'Kenrick & Sons' (Hastings Museum).

Shaped box iron showing the inner slug (Hastings Museum)

irons

The sad irons were made in different sizes, to give different weights, and the sizes were marked on the iron, ranging between 1 and 12, although the number 14 can occasionally be found. However, manufacturers did not work to a standard sizing and irons of the same number could vary quite considerably. The smallest iron was about 4 inches (10 cm) in length, the largest about 10 inches (25½ cm) long.

In 1871, Mary Florence Potts patented her famous iron, known as 'Mrs Potts Patent' or 'Mrs Potts Cold Handled Sad Iron'. These were sold in sets of three and each one had a detachable wooden handle. This was unclipped and removed while the iron was being heated and therefore always remained cool to the touch. The base plate was also detachable and was pointed at both ends for maximum efficiency. This proved so popular that it was still being made in the mid-20th century.

Ever inventive, the Victorians produced the fuelled iron in the late 1800s. Various substances were used such as paraffin, petroleum, naphtha, alcohol and methylated spirits. Coal-gas could be fed into the iron by means of a flexible tube, and the burners then lighted. Alternatively, a hollow iron was placed on to a burning gas jet.

Electric irons were developed in the 1880s, but these were heavy to use and expensive to buy.

Goose irons; £20–£25.

Group of pattern or leaf irons used for embossing velvet; £100+ each.

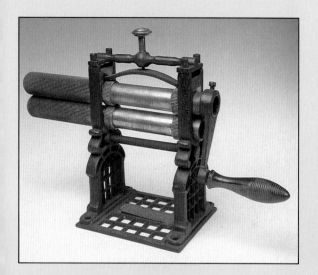

Crimping machine marked
'E & T Clark's Warranted'.
Height 10 inches (25.4 cm).

Specialist irons included the Italian or 'Tally' iron. This consisted
of a hollow tube that was heated by the insertion of a rod. It was
mounted on a stem, sometimes S-shaped, and the ribbons and
bows, frills and ruffles were passed firmly over the tube to smooth
out the creases. Goffering and crimping irons were also used for
dealing with frills and ruffs. The goffering machine consisted of a
number of small ribbed metal tubes arranged on a mangle-like
machine and rotated with a handle. Goffering tongs were made in a
style similar to the curling tongs used on hair.

The tailor's goose was an elongated iron which had a long goose-
neck handle, while milliners and hatters used small oblong box irons
with extended handles for smoothing the nap on hats. Milliners also
used double-ended irons for ironing the crown of a bonnet.

Sad irons made in cast iron are easily found and will cost from
about £5–£10 upwards. Those bearing the name of the
manufacturer are sought after, as are those of very small or very
large size. Box irons will start at about £20–£30, although those with
wooden handles, a brass face plate and complete with an iron slug
will be about £50–£100. A charcoal or ember iron will be £15–£20
upwards.

(See also IRON STANDS.)

· IRON · STANDS ·

Once the smoothing iron had been heated, it was important that it was placed on a heat-resistant stand to prevent scorching the ironing table in between use. Early stands were made in brass, either hand-worked from sheet brass, or cast in a bewildering variety of designs. Cast iron stands came later, at the beginning of the 19th century.

Iron stand in cast iron, intricately designed (Hastings Museum).

The spade or heart shape of the stand echoed that of the iron, although some were made in horseshoe, round or crescent shape, or could resemble a pair of compasses. They also had an integral carrying or hanging handle which was occasionally made in turned wood or ebony, and had three supporting feet. The stands varied in length between a tiny 4½-inch to a large 10½-inch (11.5–27 cm) size.

The pierced and openwork designs were incredibly varied. Scrollwork and geometric motifs of open circles, chevrons and triangles alternated with daisy petal and leaf patterns.

Cast brass and cast iron stands were often embossed, allowing for an even greater flexibility of pattern. Some were commemorative, marking royal jubilees and coronations; some were patriotic, showing a soldier from World War I with the caption, 'A Gentleman in Kharki' [sic]; while others bore the Masonic emblems of star and compass.

Some stands are being reproduced from the original moulds, so it is important to buy only from a reputable dealer until the necessary experience is acquired to be able to tell the difference.

Cast iron stands begin at about £10–£20; those in brass will be £20–£50 upwards.

(See also TRIVETS.)

·JELLY·
·MOULDS·

Jellies were originally savoury meat
jellies and aspics, made with the
gelatine obtained from cows' feet and
sheep's heads, flavoured with meat
extract. Hartshorn jelly was also savoury
and the gelatine for this was made from
shavings of the antlers of deer. Later,
isinglass, which was made from fish,
gave jellies improved setting qualities.
By the 18th century, sugar was being
imported in great quantity from the
West Indies and was widely available,
and so sweet jellies came into favour.
These were flavoured with fruit juices,
nuts and various wines. Colour was
obtained naturally: saffron gave a deep
yellow shade, spinach provided green,
while scarlet and carmine were obtained
from the cochineal insect.

At first, jellies were served in
individual dishes or glasses and it was
not until the mid-18th century that the
moulds became larger. They were
initially made in white salt-glazed
stoneware, recognisable by its orange-
peel finish, and had an interior pattern
of fish, melons, suns, moons, stars and
shells. Other moulds had spirally fluted
sides. Some moulds were flat-bottomed,
but others had curved bowl-shaped

Selection of pottery
moulds; £20–£70+.

Group of copper jelly moulds, showing the imaginative designs used.

exteriors and these were set on small pegged feet for stability.

At about this time, Josiah Wedgwood introduced his two-part moulds made in his famous cream-coloured 'Queen's Ware'. The outer hollow part of the mould was inverted and set in a supporting base of sand before being filled with clear jelly. The inner 'core', which was decorated with hand-painted designs in coloured enamels, was then inserted, the excess jelly running out through the holes at its base. When the jelly had set, the outer mould was removed to reveal the inner core which now glistened and magnified the pattern beneath. The jelly was not intended for consumption but was made as a table centre-piece to surprise and amaze the dinner guests. Shapes of the inner core varied from a tall four-sided obelisk to a wide triangular wedge, and a slim inverted 'ice-cream' cone. Designs included garlands of flowers and bunches of fruit or vegetables.

From the 19th century onwards, moulds were made in a variety of ceramic materials, such as pearlware, creamware and earthenware. Makers included Copeland & Garrett, Davenport, Booths, Minton, Maling, Shelley, and Grimwades. The range of interior designs was enormous. Fruit such as pineapples, grapes, plums and

The 'Paragon' Blanc-Mange & Jelly Moull (sic) made by Grimwades and advertising their 'Quick-Cooker'.

strawberries were popular. Shells,
dolphins, swans, the Prince of Wales's
feathers, and sheaves of corn were
among the many varied designs. Some
moulds were stepped so that different
colours could be layered attractively. In
the 1930s, 'Jazz Jelly', made in stripes,
was favoured.

Ring moulds with the pattern on both
interior and exterior surfaces were
made. These could be used for both
sweet and savoury jellies, the central
'hole' being filled with fruit and/or
whipped cream or with a salad and
mayonnaise.

Blancmange moulds closely
resembled jelly moulds, but were
shallower and had a wider rim. Many of
these were issued by manufacturers of
cornflour powder, such as Brown &
Polson, and these advertising moulds
can be found with a recipe printed on
the exterior.

Copper jelly moulds date from about
1830 and can also be found in a variety
of shapes and sizes. The moulds were

Collection of miniature
copper aspic moulds;
£30–£40 each.

j

On the left mould:
er Brown & Polson's "Patent Cornflour
pint Milk
Tea-spoonful Butter or Margarine
pinch of Salt
sugar according to taste

Mix cornflour to a smooth cream with
the milk. Heat the rest of the milk to
point. Remove from fire. Pour the
flour slowly into the heated milk, stirring
ously. Add the butter and salt
for ten minutes, stirring all the time
into this mould and allow to cool.
When cold turn out and serve

On the right mould:
CORN FLOUR BLANC-MANGE.
BROWN & POLSON'S.

Mix (5 table spoonsful filled level) Corn Flour, 7 tablesp.
1 Pint (3 breakfast cups quite full) good sweet milk.
Mix Corn Flour well with a little of this milk.
Heat the rest of the milk to boiling point.
Pour Corn Flour into heated milk, stirring well.
Add half a teaspoonful of butter.
Boil and stir well for 10 minutes (by the clock)
Flavour and flavour, if desired, but served with
jam or marmalade is better.
Pour into mould, and cool.
Boil gently, in mould if desired, before the fire or in some
turn out and serve cold, or hot

Blancmange moulds by
Brown & Polson's
(manufacturers of
cornflour).
LEFT: Shaped mould;
£15–£20.
RIGHT: Plain mould;
£35–£40.

tinned inside to prevent verdigris
poisoning and this gives the interior a
dull grey look. Early moulds were hand-
beaten into shape, but from about 1860,
they were machine pressed. They were
generally larger than their ceramic
counterparts and designs included
crescent moons and stars, smiling suns,
melons and massive piles of fruit and
flowers. The malleable metal lent itself
well to being pressed out in the popular
swirled, fluted, turreted and castellated
shapes.

Britannia metal (q.v.) was widely
used between about 1830–1880. This
was superior to copper in that it was a
non-poisonous metal, but if not polished
regularly, it became discoloured and the
metal oxidised. This led to the interior
becoming rough and pitted and useless
for slipping out jellies.

Glass moulds date from the turn of
the century. Easily made by machine
pressing, glass was an ideal medium for
moulding, giving crisp clear details to
the jelly. Anchors, turrets and castles
were all favourites, with animals such as
the rabbit and tortoise being used in the
1940s/1950s.

Ceramic jelly moulds sometimes carry
the maker's mark. This will help date

the mould, and will enhance the value. Severe interior staining will detract from the piece. Early copper moulds were heavier than their later counterparts and very thin, light moulds should be avoided as these are probably reproduction. Check for splits and bad dents; small dents are acceptable. If wanted for use, then the moulds should be re-tinned professionally for safety's sake.

Very early creamware moulds will cost between £50–£100; those marked with the maker's name, such as Shelley or Grimwades, will be about £15–£40. Unmarked moulds cost about £20–£30, but much depends on the interior pattern. A Brown & Polson advertising blancmange mould will be between £15–£40.

Early copper moulds of castellated form will be about £100–£150; a melon-shaped mould will be about £60 upwards. Small fish-shaped moulds will be £30–£40; those of larger size about £60–£100. Glass moulds are relatively cheap and will be between about £5–£15, depending on age and style.

Glass jelly moulds; £7–£10.

· KETTLES ·
COPPER & BRASS

Spouted containers suspended over the fire to heat water have been used since the Middle Ages. They were based largely on the cauldron and generally had two spouts so that they could be tilted either way for pouring. In the 17th century, tea became a popular drink and it became necessary to have a more easily manageable vessel which would boil a smaller amount of water. A serpentine spout directed the hot water accurately, as well as allowing the steam to escape without the kettle boiling over.

These early kettles were made of silver. Its heat-conducting qualities were excellent and, as tea was a rich man's drink, a silver kettle was affordable.

When tea became cheaper and available to the lower classes, a different metal had to be found to replace the expensive silver. Copper also had high heat conductivity and soon almost every home had a copper kettle. Brass kettles were less efficient as regards heat conductivity, and more costly to buy, but these disadvantages were largely outweighed by the attractiveness of the metal.

Early kettles were generally of a circular shape, flat-topped or pot-bellied, with a flat bottom suitable for standing on the newly developed hob grate. Handles were also made of copper or brass, and these were movable in early models, as some housewives still hung their kettles over an open fire to boil. In the later Victorian era, the handles became fixed and the user was protected from burnt hands by turned wooden grips fitted on to the metal.

Copper and brass kettles should be checked for splits and wear. Seams that

Brass kettle of stylised shape, with a cane handle; £38–£40.

Copper kettle of traditional shape with an acorn finial on the lid. Height 11 inches (28 cm)

k

started to leak may have been clumsily
soldered. The riveting should also be
checked as this is an indication of age.
Check handles for replacement. These
kettles are being widely reproduced so
buy only from a reputable dealer.

Prices will vary according to the age
and condition of the kettle, and the
attractiveness of the shape. Generally,
they cost about £50–£100; an early
Victorian kettle may cost £100–£150.

· KEYS · & · LOCKS ·

There has been a need to lock things up
for privacy or safety since about
2000 BC, and massive wooden keys
made by the Egyptians have been
found, dating from this period. These
early keys resembled a bent tongue of
wood with a row of raised pegs at one
end, and were the forerunners of the
modern cylinder lock. By about 300 BC
Egyptian keys had become 'L' shaped,
and this shape was also used by the
Romans for their bronze and iron keys
in the 6th century, although they also
had spade-shaped keys which had
pierced maze-like patterns.

The general pattern of keys changed
very little between the 16th and 20th
centuries. They consisted of a ward (the

Late 17th-century key
(Hasting Museum).

Various 19th and 20th
century door and box
keys.

LEFT to RIGHT: Large
latch key;
key to an iron chest at
Hatton Church 1832;
bronze key of No 34
Martello Tower c.1805,
marked with an arrow and
WD on the back
(Hastings Museum).

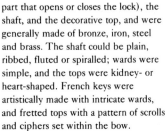

part that opens or closes the lock), the
shaft, and the decorative top, and were
generally made of bronze, iron, steel
and brass. The shaft could be plain,
ribbed, fluted or spiralled; wards were
simple, and the tops were kidney- or
heart-shaped. French keys were
artistically made with intricate wards,
and fretted tops with a pattern of scrolls
and ciphers set within the bow.

Mortice locks came into being in about
1760 and these operated on the sliding
bolt principle. In 1784, Joseph Bramah
invented the lever lock, and Chubb
perfected his 'detector' lock in 1818.
The rim lock appeared in about 1830,
the Yale lock was invented in 1848.

Keys vary enormously in price, with
modern keys costing just a few pence,
and elaborate 16th- and 17th-century
keys fetching hundreds of pounds.
Victorian keys will cost from about £5
upwards depending on size and design.

· KNIFE · & ·
· CUTLERY ·
· BOXES ·

Knives were contained in special cases
from the 16th century and these
became popular in Great Britain in the
early 18th century. At first they were
tall upright wooden boxes with a curved
serpentine front and a sloping lid. This
made it possible to see clearly the
contents which were placed in a series
of 'cells' formed by many velvet-
covered wooden partitions. The cases
were made in polished wood such as
walnut or were covered in shagreen
(q.v.). They were sometimes inlaid with
various coloured woods or embellished
with ornate silver mounts. Japanned
metal boxes were also made and these
were often hand-painted.

Late Victorian cutlery trays
in pine; £15–£20 each.

The knife vase was introduced in the late 1700s and it is thought to have been designed by Robert Adams. The lid of this urn-like container lifted off to reveal a series of openings arranged in decreasing circles. The cutlery was placed in its appropriate slot, knives with their blades down, spoons with their bowls uppermost.

Cutlery boxes date from the Victorian era and were generally used to carry the cutlery to the table, a well as for storage. The open tray-like box was made in oak or pine, and had three or four divisions. A simple cut-out handle was set centrally. More elaborate were the boxes with two sloping lids and brass handles. These were baize or felt lined and the spoons and forks were neatly held in slotted grooves, with the knives placed in slots contained in both lids.

Good quality cutlery was sold in canteens. These oak or mahogany boxes were lined with baize and the cutlery was set out in rows. There were often two tiers, with the top tier taking the form of a lift-out tray; alternatively, the base consisted of a drawer which could be pulled out only when the lid of the canteen was opened.

Early Georgian knife boxes and vases are prohibitively priced, costing

Baize-lined cutlery box with brass carrying handle; £30–£40 (without cutlery).

between £500–£1500. Simple cutlery trays are at the bottom end of the market, and will cost about £5–£15, depending on condition. Lidded carrying boxes will be about £35–£60, while canteens cost about £10–£25 upwards depending on whether they are made of oak or mahogany. Two-tier boxes with a drawer will be about £50 upwards. (All prices exclude cutlery.)

· KNIFE ·
· CLEANERS ·

Until the advent of stainless steel, knives were prone to both rust and staining. They were cleaned by first scouring with washing soda and hot water, and then polished by 'stropping' against the knife board which was covered with leather or an india rubber compound.

In 1870, Kent's produced a rotary knife cleaning machine. This consisted of a large circular wooden drum which was mounted vertically on a cast iron stand. The knives were slotted into the apertures set at intervals around the drum, an abrasive emery powder was poured in, and the drum rotated energetically. As the knives went round, they hit against a series of leather leaves which 'stropped' and polished them.

Knife cleaner by George Kent Ltd., London. Height 18 inches (45.7 cm); £80–£120.

Knife cleaner of simple design. Height 8 inches (20.3 cm); £40–£80.

Alternatively, the knives were slapped against alternating pads of felt and bristle attachments. As the knives were taken out, they were drawn against brushes which dusted off the abrasive powder.

The drum-like knife cleaner was efficient but it had one great disadvantage in that the vigorous polishing wore down the blades of the knives very quickly. Spong produced their 'Servant's Friend' which used a leather disc rather than leaves and this could take up to four knives. They also made the 'Lady's Knife Cleaner' which operated like a press, the knife being drawn between two leather leaves held down under pressure.

But by the end of the 19th century, Knight's patent knife cleaner came on the market. It resembled a small mangle, and the knife blades were polished by placing them between two rubber rollers which were then rotated. Some took only one knife, while others could cope with up to four knives. This type of knife cleaner proved popular and, as late as 1929, the Besway Knife Cleaner was being sold at Harrod's.

The mangle-type cleaners can be found for about £20–£40 upwards; the large drum cleaners will start at about £100–£150.

·KNIFE·RESTS·

Made in the 18th and 19th centuries, pairs of knife rests were used to protect the tablecloth from being soiled when the master of the house rested from carving the roast meat. They were made in silver, silver plate, pewter, base metal, ceramic and glass, and rather resembled miniature dumb-bells, having a central bar with two supporting ends, often ornamental.

Glass knife rests are quite commonly seen and can be attractively cut and faceted. Metal rests could have knobbed crucifix ends, or could be more elaborate with mother-of-pearl bars and embossed silver mounts. Ceramic rests were more pillow-shaped and transfer-printed in blue and white, or decorated with hand-painted flowers.

When buying glass rests, check carefully for any chips; examine ceramic rests for cracks. Ensure that metal or silver mounts are secure and not damaged.

Prices can be quite low, especially if buying at auction. A plated pair will cost from about £5–£10; those in mother-of-pearl with plated silver mounts will be about £15–£20. Glass rests will start at about the same price as plated ones, but this price will depend on the complexity of cutting. Ceramic rests are more unusual and will start at about £15–£20.

Pair of knife rests in mother-of-pearl with silver-plated end supports; £15–£20.

· LADLES · & · · SKIMMERS ·

Long-handled metal ladles were used in the kitchen for stirring and doling out food and liquids from the cauldron which hung over the open fire. The handles were long from necessity, otherwise the cook was in danger of being scorched or even burned. The majority of these ladles were made in brass, although iron and pewter were also used. Copper gave rise to verdigris poisoning and so was best avoided in cooking unless the surfaces that touched the food could be protectively tinned.

Ladles with shorter handles and with round, flat, pierced pans were called 'skimmers' and were used in the dairy to skim the cream from the surface of the milk. Any milk also taken up would drain through the holes.

Toddy spoons or ladles were small and short-handled and were made in wood, horn or metal. These were used for transferring the hot toddy into a suitable drinking vessel.

Small china and pottery ladles were originally part of a dinner set and would have been placed in the tureens, especially the small round tureen made for sauces. These ceramic ladles can be most decorative, and would have the same pattern as that which decorated the service. The pattern is usually on the handle, and on good examples on the interior and/or rim of the bowl.

Brass ladles and pierced skimmers will cost about £30–£50, depending on length. Small toddy ladles in horn and wood will be about £10–£20 upwards, depending on age. China ladles vary in price according to the transfer printed pattern, but fairly plain ladles will start at about £5–£10; more ornate varieties will be £10–£30 or more.

· LAVATORY ·
· CHAIN · PULLS ·

In the 1870s, the high-level cistern was introduced into water closets. This had a siphon flush which was operated by pulling a long chain. To make it easier for the user, chain pulls were fitted, and these were made in wood, ceramic and Bakelite.

Wooden examples were often decoratively turned and would sometimes bear the message 'Pull and let go'. China pulls would also have the same message, or would perhaps be printed with the name of the owner of the property. Manufacturers often marked chain pulls with their trademark or with an advertising slogan. Some were decorated in a floral pattern.

Chain pulls need searching for at antiques fairs as they are not always immediately recognisable for what they are. Prices start from about £5–£10 for the wooden variety; £10–£15 upwards for china examples.

· LEMON ·
· SQUEEZERS ·

Early squeezers were made of hardwood, since metal was discoloured by the acid in the juice, and could be of various styles. The simplest, known as a lemon reamer, was shaped roughly like a pine cone with a handle. The body was grooved and the squeezer was pushed into the halved fruit and twisted to extract the juice.

The two-handled squeezer operated rather like a pair of nutcrackers (q.v.) and had a depression on one side into which the halved lemon was fitted, and a grooved protuberance on the other side. When the handles were brought together, the juice was squeezed out.

Later models were more bat-shaped and had china inserts that could be removed for washing.

Lemon squeezers were also made in glass and china, with slightly larger examples being used for oranges. The halved fruit was pushed down on to the raised centre and the juice ran down into the waiting integral saucer. Some ceramic squeezers were set on small bowls or jugs and were perforated to retain the pips, but to allow the juice to trickle through.

Wooden squeezers will start at about £15–£30, as will those with china inserts. Reamers cost about £20–£30. Glass orange and china lemon squeezers will be about £10–£15.

LEFT to RIGHT: Large glass orange squeezer £10; wood and ceramic lemon squeezer £26; 'Crown Devon' ceramic orange squeezer £10; plastic lemon squeezer £7.

· LETTER · RACKS ·
& *HOLDERS*

With the advent of the postal service in the mid-19th century, every household received letters and these were placed in a rack for safe keeping. These were made in brass, papier-mâché or wood and the simplest design consisted of an angled 'pocket' set against a back plate. They were intended to be hung on the wall and were attractively decorated with embossed patterns (brass), hand-painted flowers and designs (papier-

Hanging rack in wood and stamped sheet brass, having a pattern of urns and flowers.

Wooden letter rack with copper decoration; £25–£30.

mâché), inlay, marquetry or pokerwork (wood), or the word 'Letters'. Shapes varied, too, from the simple envelope style to horseshoe or heart shapes. Larger racks were free standing and intended for desks where they also doubled as stationery boxes. These were also made in wood, brass or papier mâché, and were partitioned to take the various sizes of paper.

Small individual letter holders made of metal or brass were also intended for the desk, and used a spring clip to hold the letter in place. These often took the form of a hand emerging from a cuff, and birds' heads were also very popular. The plainer type resembled an elongated bulldog clip and were heavily embossed with scrolls and acanthus leaves, or were monogrammed with the owner's initials.

Brass 'horseshoe' letter rack; £30–£35.

Wall hanging racks can be found quite cheaply from about £15–£20 upwards. Brass examples should be examined carefully for signs of age as new ones are still being made. Wooden racks will also start at the same price. Plain metal holders with a spring clip will start at about £10; those in brass featuring a hand, about 4 to 6 inches (10–15½ cm) in length will start at about £50, while birds' heads vary between about £70–£250, depending on how realistic they are.

· LETTER · · SCALES · & · · BALANCES ·

Introduced in the 1840s, letter scales fall into two categories: the balance scale which operated on a see-saw principle, and the spring scale, although a small steelyard scale, in a very ornate style, was also available.

The balance scale was made of brass and usually plain in style, relying on the ornamental base or plinth for decorative appeal. The base could be made of polished wood, left plain or brass-mounted, inlaid marble, onyx, alabaster, silver, silver plate, brass or copper. The accompanying brass weights ranged between ½ ounce to 4 ounces (14–113.4 g) and were set in recesses in the base.

There were two types of spring scale. One, also called the 'candlestick' scale, consisted of a cylindrical column, set on a wide base and having a slender rod rising from the main part of the stem which had a graduated scale of weights and a pointer. The letter was placed on the round flat plate which was fixed to the sprung stem, and the pointer indicated its exact weight.

The other type, oblong in shape with

Letter scales with graduated quadrant indicating 0–2 oz, possibly Royal Mail.

GPO letter scales in brass and wood; £120.

a curved calibrated front, appeared in the late 19th/early 20th century. The letter holder was also oblong. These later scales were generally made in base metal.

The steelyard scale consisted of a base on which two pillars or rods supported a calibrated beam. A metal counterpoise was moved along the beam to indicate the weight of the letter which had been placed in the pan that was suspended from one end of the beam.

If buying a balance scale, ensure that it is antique and not a reproduction. Highly polished brasswork and a varnished base are giveaways, as are thin supporting pinions.

Plain balance scales with a polished oak or mahogany base start at about £50–£100, but will cost about £100–£1000 or more if the base is ornate. Candlestick-type spring scales will be about £100 or more, while an ornate steelyard balance will be £500–£750.

· LLOYD · LOOM ·
· FURNITURE ·

Up until the early 20th century, wicker furniture had been made by hand, a laborious and labour-intensive process. In 1917, Marshall B. Lloyd, an American, invented a machine capable of weaving a fabric that closely resembled wicker.

The fabric, made of twisted paper or wood pulp fibre, was reinforced with steel wire for durability. The frame for the furniture was steamed and bent to the required shape, and the woven 'fibre' attached. It was then sized, restretched and oven-dried, and sometimes finished off with a woven braid. When completed, the piece was spray-painted in pastel shades of green,

Occasional table (minus glass top); £30–£40.

blue, orange or cream.

In 1922, the process was franchised to a British manufacturer, W. Lusty & Sons Ltd. Initially, items such as linen baskets for use in the bathroom were produced, as well as small tables, some with glass tops fixed with chromed clips, and suites of furniture comprising a pair of round-backed armchairs and a two-seater settee.

The British loom furniture was made in a range of 36 colours, which included gold and silver, and some pieces also had a delicate edging of gold spray. Soon, Lusty & Son were producing garden furniture, bedside cabinets, pedestal cupbards with drawers, hat stands, waste paper baskets and even a writing desk.

Early Lloyd loom made by W. Lusty bore a metal label marked with the date of manufacture, although over the years these labels have frequently become detached and are missing.

Bedroom chair with upholstered seat; £60–£80.

Lloyd loom furniture can be cleaned by wiping it with a damp cloth; dirt and dust lodged in the crevices of the weave can be removed with the aid of a toothbrush, used dry or dipped in warm soapy water. The piece should never be soaked with water as this will damage the weave and unravel the fibres. Paint stripper should never be used either as this will also damage the weave.

When buying, avoid items that show any damage to the weave, or that have been over-painted in unsuitable colours.

Prices will be reasonable for small items such as flat-topped linen baskets which will cost from about £10–£20 in auction; those with a domed lid will be about £20–£50. A cushioned bedroom chair with Queen Anne-style legs will be about £50–£100; an armchair with rounded back will cost about the same. Glass-topped tables start at £50–£100.

Linen basket with domed lid; £20–£25.

· MEASURES ·

The oldest measure of capacity is the bushel, which was used as much as a thousand years ago; the term, along with the half-bushel and peck, was in use until January 1969. Early measures were made in leather or wood, with pewter becoming popular in the 15th century.

Most unlidded tankards, known as mugs, found today date from after about 1800, and come in measures of quarts, pints and half-pints. They were made in pewter, brass, tin, pottery, earthenware, stoneware and glass. Earthenware measures were marked by stencilling on the side, usually near the rim or handle. A steel stencil was placed in position and the glaze removed by a powerful jet of sand thus etching the mark indelibly.

Glass was stencilled after about 1880, and usually carries a date number, plus the inspector's district number. Previously, glass had been stamped.

Measures were used not only for liquids, but also for foodstuffs such as peas, seeds and small shellfish like prawns. The use of wood for liquids was banned in the 18th century but it was still used for dry goods; large 'cran' measures were used for fish.

Apart from mugs and tankards, jug-like measures were also used, which

Large ironstone jug, graduated for pints and quarts; £15–£20. Enamel ½-pint measure; £5–£10. Blue and white transfer-printed ½-pint measures; £25–£40.

were often made in copper. Conical in shape, with the base wider than the neck which was lipped for ease of pouring, the jugs ranged between a ½ pint size (0.3 l) and a massive 5 gallon (22.7 l) version, used commercially. Smaller, straight-sided aluminium or enamelled jugs and mugs were made for household use in the 20th century, usually for liquids; these have a graduated scale embossed into the metal or printed on to the interior surface.

Advertising measures were made in pottery, usually by dairies who wanted to promote their milk and/or cream.

Prices will start at about £5–£10 for an enamel measure; about £15–£20 upwards for pottery examples. Victorian wooden measures of a quart, pint and half-pint will be £20–£30; copper conical jugs will vary according to size, but a complete set of nine will be over £1000. An advertising measure will be about £30–£35.

·MENU· ·HOLDERS·

During the late Victorian era, no formal dinner table would have been complete without menu holders. They varied in size from small individual holders into which the handwritten menu was slotted, to larger ceramic 'menus' with a plain surface on to which the hostess

Celluloid menu holder
c.1930; £15–£20.

would write the various dishes the guests would be having.

Small holders were made in silver, silver plate, ivory, china and glass. These ranged from plain circular discs made in metal which gripped the menu, to glass holders made in artistic leaf or flower shapes. Porcelain holders were made in the form of scallop shells, while Royal Doulton produced small mice playing musical instruments in stoneware. Novelty holders appeared in the 1920s, and Goebel's produced a small scarlet Scottie dog set on a black base.

The ceramic 'menus' were oblong, supported by a small china strut at the back. The word 'menu' would be printed in perhaps black or gold, and the plain surface would be edged or bordered with a scroll or garland of flowers.

Individual menu holders can be found relatively cheaply, with small china examples starting at £10–£15. Decorative glass will be about £40–£50 upwards for a pair, while silver-plated holders will start at about £40–£50, depending on size. Ceramic 'menus' will cost about £15–£30 upwards, depending on the amount of decoration.

Three from a set of eight celluloid place markers c.1937; £85 the set.

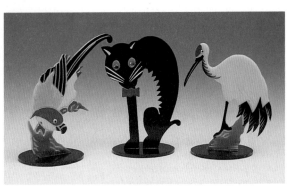

· MINCERS ·
& MINCING MACHINES

Until the mid-19th century, food had been minced by chopping finely. With the advent of the sausage and general mincing machine made by Spong, the housewife's life was made much easier. The cast iron mincer consisted of a chute or hopper into which the meat was fed. This chute led into a drum-shaped cavity which contained the tinned iron propeller, driven by rotating an outside handle, and the steel blades set in racks. There was an adjustable slide for cutting coarsely or finely, and a nozzle out of which the minced meat emerged. Some mincers came complete with a pierced cone which could be attached to the machine to feed the sausage meat into the skin.

'The No 1 Siddons Mincer' for kitchen table top use.

Spong made several sizes of mincer ranging from 0 to 10. The smallest was 'The Minnie Mincer', costing eight shillings and sixpence (42½ pence), which was intended to be clamped to the edge of the kitchen table. The largest was 'The Monster Mincer', costing £35, which had a heavy cast iron base and weighed about 11 hundredweight (558.8 kg).

The cast iron mincers were enamelled, and the handles had turned wooden grips. In the 1890s aluminium replaced cast iron.

Small household mincers do not cost a great deal and an enamelled version can be found for about £5–£10 upwards. A large commercial variety will be £50 and more.

· MONEY · BOXES ·

Although used by the Romans in the form of sealed terracotta jars, the money box did not become popular in Europe

Pottery money box marked Samuel Jasper, Brighton 1801.

TOP: Wooden money boxes, one in the shape of a barrel; £10–£20. Tinplate and brass boxes; £7–£20.

until the 17th century. The majority of those seen today, however, date from the late 18th/early 19th century when small ceramic cottages, castles and other buildings were made.

The Victorian era saw wooden money boxes in both inlaid Tunbridge ware and transfer-decorated Mauchline ware, and these were designed as barrels, brass-bound caskets, or books. Cast iron boxes were made to resemble animal or human heads with open mouths. American cast iron boxes of 1870 also used this form of encouraging children to save. An outstretched hand took the coin and it was mechanically raised and tilted into the open mouth. The Americans also produced other novelty money boxes which operated automatically when a coin was placed on the waiting surface. A negroid head would 'swallow' the coin while rolling his eyes; a baby monkey was rescued from a lion by shooting a coin into the latter's mouth. A dentist delivered a coin into his patient's mouth at the touch of a button, while, by pressing his foot, a Unionist soldier from the Civil

Metal money box c.1920 showing a bear wearing headphones and sitting on a radio (Hastings Museum).

War would shoot the coin into a hole in the tree opposite him.

Towards the end of the century, money boxes were made in cast alloys which were then painted or given a brass finish. Bears, boots, barrels and banks were made in brass; pillar boxes, safes and books were in brightly painted tinplate. Sweet and biscuit manufacturers also made tins (q.v.) which, after the contents had been eaten, could be used as money boxes. China and pottery pigs, regarded as symbols of prosperity, came in all sizes, as did hens seated on their nests. Bears, rabbits, beehives and even fish were popular.

The mechanical negro's head from America is now being reproduced, and if convincingly 'aged' can deceive the unwary. Original cast iron mechanical money boxes can cost as much as £500, more if rare examples, so care must be taken when buying.

China cottages will cost about £80–£100; more if from the 18th or early 19th century. Plain wooden boxes are about £15–£30; inlaid or transfer-printed examples about twice this price. Tinplate boxes vary enormously in style and design, and the price varies accordingly. There is no set price band.

Double gourd-like money box with openings for both small and large coins.

n

A Silver napkin ring, hallmarked Birmingham 1922; £10–£15.

· NAPKIN ·
· RINGS ·

Before the start of the 19th century, napkins were generally placed on the table artfully folded in a variety of shapes, and no napkin was ever used twice. As laundry costs rose, napkins were rolled up after the meal and placed into a cylindrical band for re-use. By the 1850s napkin rings were being used more widely, and by the 1870s they were seen on almost every table.

Silver, silver-plated, EPNS (q.v.) and brass rings were popular but as the tourist industry grew, they were made as souvenirs in ivory, bone, horn, tortoiseshell, and wood decorated with pokerwork, inlaid mosaics (Tunbridge ware), and transfer pictures (Mauchline ware), and, in the 20th century, they were made in brightly coloured plastic, pottery and china.

Metal rings were circular, oval, square or octagonal. They could be initialled, monogrammed or numbered, and could resemble a belt with buckle, or be hinged. They could be embossed with all manner of designs, have elegant engine-turned decoration, be pierced in a pattern of birds, fruit and flowers, or in series of Gothic arches. The Art Nouveau period saw napkin rings embossed with Celtic motifs, bands of Tudor roses or leaves with whiplash

LEFT: Painted wooden napkin ring; £3.
RIGHT: Wooden ring carved with a design of fruit and leaves and bearing a monogram; £6–£8.

Mauchline ware black transfer-printed napkin rings.
LEFT: A view of the Ruins of Brambletye, East Grinstead; £8–£10.
RIGHT: The Esplanade at Bognor; £5–£6.

tendrils.

In the 1920s/30s, the Art Deco movement gave rise to novelty ceramic napkin rings and one can find clowns supporting the circular band, policemen straddling it and crinoline ladies standing in front of it. Plastic napkin holders were made in bright colours in the shape of dogs, cats, chickens, ducks and other animals.

Single napkin rings in silver will cost about £15–£25 upwards, depending on age and style, with those of exotic or extravagant style or by a famous silversmith being as much as £200. Sets of rings will start at about £50 for those of plain style. Silver-plated rings will start at about £5–£10, but only buy these if the plating is still good. Art Nouveau rings will cost from about £40–£50 upwards. Art Deco ceramic napkin holders will be about £20–£25 upwards, depending on the style and novelty aspect, with some reaching as much as £100. A boxed set of Bakelite rings in various colours from the same period will be about £15–£20.

LEFT: Metal napkin ring with enamelled *cloisonné* design; £10–£12.
RIGHT: Wooden ring with transfer-printed tartan design; £5–£10.

·NUTCRACKERS·

Nutcrackers of screw type, the top one shaped like a squirrel; £60–£100.

It was traditional for the Victorians to serve nuts in their shells at the end of a meal, and nutcrackers were provided for the guests.

These fall into two types: those operating on a screw principle where the nut was held in a circular opening and a screw was turned to bring sufficient pressure on the nut to crack it, and the hinged variety of the 'jaw' type which operated by applying sufficient pressure to the handles to crush the shell.

The screw-type nutcrackers can be found with plain round rings, or perhaps with the ring ornamented by a gripping hand.

The hinged nutcrackers are more commonly available and these can be found in both wood such as yew, walnut, boxwood and fruitwood, or metal, such as cast iron, steel or brass. Some were dual-purpose, having nut-pick handles for coaxing the nut out of its shell.

Wooden hinged nutcrackers could be made in novelty shapes, perhaps having a grinning man's head with a hinged jaw at the business end. Metal examples were made in the shapes of dogs or crocodiles, the nut being inserted between the jaws.

Hinged nutcrackers in brass, steel and cast iron; £7–£15.

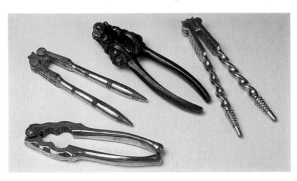

Wooden nutcrackers of the screw type will be about £60–£100, while wooden hinged nutcrackers will be about £35–£40 for those depicting a man's head. Novelty metal nutcrackers from about 1850 will be from £30–£35, but the later the period, the cheaper the nutcracker.

· NUTMEG · · GRATERS ·

The nutmeg is a small hard nut which, when grated, is used as a spice in both food and drink. It has been known in Europe since medieval times and in the second half of the 17th century was used widely to flavour hot mulled wines, punch and toddies.

Early pocket graters were usually less then 3 inches (8 cm) long, were made in silver and consisted of a cylindrical silver rasp set in a cylindrical capped case. The heart- or teardrop-shaped nutmeg grater made its appearance between about 1705–30. Acorn graters, which unscrewed into three pieces to house the roughened iron or steel rasp, the spice and the whole nut, date from about 1730–55. Egg- and barrel-shaped containers made their appearance in about 1750–60, to be followed in about 1800 by the hydrant and oval, both of which had pull-off lids.

The cylinder was revived in about 1780 and remained popular until about 1820. It was now fitted with a hinged lid and had a cut-away side into which the grater was fitted. This rasp was covered by a hinged flap which was further secured by the top lid. Boxes also made their appearance at around this time and were mainly oval in shape, although square, rectangular with cut corners, and octagonal boxes were also made. These later nutmeg graters were

Varied selection of nutmeg graters in both metal and wood; £5–£65.

made in silver-plate, wood, tin and japanned metal, as well as in silver.

By the 1830s, pocket nutmeg graters were going out of fashion. However, they were still used in the dining room, being set near the tantalus or drinks stand. They were also widely used in the kitchen, where they were of a larger size, ranging from 4 to 10 inches (10–25½ cm) in length. They were generally semi-circular in shape with the roughened surface being on the curved section, and having a handle for ease attached to the back plate. Nutmeg graters were also incorporated into sectioned wooden spice boxes, or could consist of a small box set on a rectangular rasp. The box was sprung and held the nut, and the spice was obtained by pushing the box up and down the rasp. This did the job neatly and quickly, and avoided the risk of scraped fingers.

Early silver nutmeg graters will cost anything between £100–£500; those in japanned metal or tin will be about £50–£100. Wooden acorn-style graters will be about £70–£120. Kitchen nutmeg graters will cost from about £10–£20.

· PAPER · KNIVES · · & · LETTER · · OPENERS ·

In the Victorian era, books and newspapers were frequently produced with uncut pages, obliging the reader to cut the pages himself. These were dealt with by use of a broad-bladed paper knife that had blunt, rounded ends. Letter openers date from about 1840 when envelopes began being used. These differ from paper knives in that they have a pointed end and the blades were often sword-like. They were also used for coping with the uncut pages of books.

Paper knives were generally made in one piece with the blade being as wide as the handle. Various materials were used, such as silver, bronze, brass, wood, bone, horn, ivory, celluloid, tortoiseshell and papier mâché.

The appeal of paper knives and letter openers lies largely in the huge variety of design of the handles. These were made in all the materials mentioned above, and also in mother-of-pearl, gold set with both precious and semi-precious stones, and carved natural stones such as jade or bloodstone.

Silver handles were heavily embossed

TOP: Commemorative Edward VII paperknife; £22.
BELOW: Three paper knives with wide blades, made in wood; £2–£10.

Metal advertising letter opener marked 'Guardian Assurance Company Ltd.'; £5–£7.

or ornately chased, and could be set with amethyst or coloured hardstones. Ivory was carved with a pattern of flowers such as chrysanthemums or peonies. Tortoiseshell and horn were silver-mounted. Wood was also carved, or could be decorated with pokerwork designs, inlaid mosaic patterns, and transfer-printed scenes. Advertising and souvenir openers were made in brass.

Prices will vary enormously for both paper knives and letter openers, depending on the material used, the design, and the age. Ornate carved ivory examples can be as much as £100–£250; Tunbridgeware knives with inlaid mosaic designs will be £25–£40, but other wooden openers with minimal decoration can be found for as little as £10–£50. Silver knives will start at about £40–£75, while silver-handled tortoiseshell openers will cost about £30–£70.

· PARASOLS ·
See Umbrellas and Parasols

· PASTRY · JIGGERS · & · CUTTERS ·

Known also as dough or pastry wheels, markers, crimpers and trimmers, the jigger consisted of a fluted and crimped solid wheel, resembling a circular grooved fan, and this was set on a small wooden handle. The cook ran this around the edge of an uncooked pie to trim it attractively. It was also used on the rolled-out pastry to cut out shapes, giving them a wavy or deckled edge. Sometimes an additional cutter was mounted on the end of the handle and when the tool was reversed, it could be used to stamp out pastry shapes.

Brass pastry jigger and stamper with an intricately turned wooden handle; £40–£50.

Pastry jiggers were made in wood, such as sycamore or boxwood, iron, steel, silver and brass. Some late-Victorian wheels were made of pottery or porcelain, and a few walrus ivory jiggers can be found.

Prices will vary according to the design of the jiggers but most will be between about £20–£50.

· PENKNIVES ·
· & · FOLDING ·
· KNIVES ·

Spring folding penknives were first made in the early 18th century when they were used for cutting quills for writing. The blades were narrow and only about 1 inch (2½ cm) long, and when closed the penknife was about 3 inches (8 cm) in length.

The folding fruit knife made its appearance a few years later in about 1780. These were made with silver or gilded blades in order to combat the corrosive action of the fruit juice. They had handles of mother-of-pearl, ivory or bone, and measured about 7 inches (18 cm) in length when open.

It is the handles of folding knives that offer the most variety to the collector,

Multi-bladed penknife with a stylised bird on the handle.

and knives made from about 1850 give
the most scope. Mother-of-pearl could
be left plain, or carved in a simple
ribbed or serrated pattern, and could
have a silver name plate, either oblong
or shield-shaped, riveted to the handle.
Silver end caps were also sometimes
added. Alternatively, the shell could be
carved in patterns of flowers and/or
scrolled foliage, with perhaps a feather-
cut end. Silver-handled knives were
embossed, engraved, bright-cut or set
with inlaid mother-of-pearl. Blades were
of silver or steel, depending on the use,
and silver examples were sometimes
engraved with patterns of stars, scrolls or
foliage, with the owner's name or initials
occasionally being featured.

Novelty knives could have handles of
brass, ivory, tortoiseshell and bone, or
one of the plastics resembling the
natural materials. The handles were
made to represent fish, perhaps,
complete with scales, or could be in the
form of the female leg, the latter being
very popular with the Victorian
gentleman.

When buying, it is important to check
that the blade is not broken or rusted,
and that the spring mechanism operates
satisfactorily with the blade retracting
completely into the handle. Mother-of-
pearl handles should be checked for
cracks, and any knives described as

p

silver should bear a hallmark (q.v.).

Prices will vary according to size, design and age. Folding knives with silver blades and mother-of-pearl handles will cost about £10–£25 for those in a plain style, more if ornately carved.

· PENS · & · PENCILS ·

The fountain pen was first manufactured in about 1832, although experiments with adding ink reservoirs to pens had taken place as early as the 17th century. However, the new pen, patented by J. J. Parker, was unsuccessful. The carbon ink used at the time tended to clog the nib, the pen was difficult to fill, and was prone to leaking. It was not until the 1880s that L. E. Waterman invented a pen with a capillary action that prevented leakage. By now, a new kind of ink had been developed, with the firm of Stephens manufacturing a chemical-based ink in both red and blue, thus doing away with the carbon ink that had consisted of soot, water and gum.

The early pens had been filled by putting the ink into the barrel by means of a dropper, but in 1908 a Mr Sheaffer patented an internal rubber ink holder which was operated by means of a lever fitted in the barrel.

Fountain pen barrels were first made of vulcanite (a vulcanised rubber) but by about 1920, barrels were being made in a variety of materials, such as Bakelite (a type of plastic), gold, silver, mother-of-pearl and even glass.

The history of the propelling pencil began in the 1820s when the 'Everpointed Pencil' was patented by Sampson Mordan in about 1825. It was very successful and his designs were to

Two fountain pens from the 1940s: the Golden Platignum, and the Summit S125.

LEFT: 'Life-Long'
propelling pencil in sterling
silver.
RIGHT: 'Yard-o-Led'
hallmarked silver pencil;
£25–£30 each.

dominate the market. The lead inside
the pencil was held in a metal tube and
was revealed by a simple sliding action
of the knob set in a slit at the side of the
barrel. Alternatively, the pencil was
equipped with a small knob which was
moved along a spiral groove or slit in the
barrel. By rotating the barrel, and
keeping the knob still, the metal tube
containing the lead was propelled to the
tip. There were refinements to these
methods but these were usually
incorporated in novelty pencils.

The size and design of Victorian
pencils varied enormously but Sampson
Mordan led the field. He specialised in
making small silver articles and some of
his pencils were only about 1 inch (2½
cm) in length. His designs included
novelty pencils which resembled pistols,
rifles and muskets, hunting horns,
whistles, feathers, a cuffed hand, golf
clubs, screws, pillar boxes and
lighthouses, and all manner of figures
ranging from children and policemen to
Egyptian mummies and Chinamen.

Materials used also varied: silver was
favourite, but propelling pencils can also
be found with cases made of ivory,
mother-of-pearl, agate, brass and various
plastics.

The most frequently found pens are
those dating from the 1920s and 1930s,
and makers include Parker, Waterman,
Swan, Croxley and Conway Stewart.
Conway Stewart are perhaps the
cheapest to buy, with prices ranging
from £10–£15 for standard pens to
about £65–£90 for their 'Dinkie' pen
made in about 1935. A Parker
Vacuumite pen from about 1940 will be

Propelling pencil c.1930
with amber-coloured
barrel and yellow metal
mounts; £10–£12.

£150–£170, and a Parker 'Lucky Curve' vest pen will be about the same price.

Propelling pencils of plain style by Mordan, dating from about 1900, will be about £10–£20; novelty pencils will cost more than double this price. Hallmarked or sterling silver pencils from about 1900 will be about £20–£30 upwards.

· PESTLES · & · · MORTARS ·

Early wooden mortar with wooden pestle.

These were used both in the kitchen and by apothecaries and herbalists, and were capable of grinding nuts, spices and dried herbs to a fine consistency.

Their use in Britain dates from the 2nd century AD when they were introduced by the Romans, although the Ancient Egyptians had them well before that date. The Roman mortar or 'mortarium' was a shallow bowl with a pouring lip. Grit was worked into the inner surface before firing in order to give a suitable grinding surface.

Early mortars from the 15th to early 18th century were generally made of bronze. They were bucket-shaped and ranged in size from a small 3 inches (7½ cm) for use domestically or by herbalists, to those of a huge 3 feet (90 cm) in height which were used in businesses or large households. These large mortars were often hewn from the trunk of a tree such as oak, elm or pine,

P

and the pestles were often capped with metal to cope with the wear of the grinding process.

From the 18th century, mortars were made in bronze, brass, bell metal or a hardwood such as lignum vitae. The shallow bowl-shaped mortar used in the Victorian kitchen was made of unglazed stoneware, with marble bowls appearing later. The pestle would be made of a material that matched the mortar, with ceramic and marble pestles being fitted with wooden handles.

Late 19th-century pestles and mortars are frequently available and a stoneware example will cost about £20–£30. A later mortar made in marble with a matching pestle will be about the same price. An early Georgian pestle and mortar in brass will be about £70–£100.

· PRESERVING · · PANS ·

Food preservation was essential to the generations who were not blessed with modern freezers, and every housewife learnt how to deal with the seasonal produce. Meat was smoked or salted, while beans and pulses were dried, as were some fruit such as apples and plums. Marmalade had been made as far back as the 12th century, while spices had long been used for preserving. Pickling in vinegar, as opposed to brine, became popular in the 17th century, and the bottling of various fruits came into vogue in the 18th century.

The Victorian housewife made jams, jellies and chutneys in large quantities, and for this she used a preserving pan. The pan could be deep or shallow, and was made of silver, brass, bronze, copper or bell metal, with later pans being made of aluminium or having

Brass berry pan, with pouring lip, and hooked swinging handle. Height 6 inches (15.2 cm), diameter 11½ inches (29.2 cm).

p

Wide copper pan with fixed carrying handles. Height 5 inches (12.7 cm), diameter 14 inches (35.5 cm).

vitreous enamelled surfaces.

Copper and brass were favourite among those who could not afford silver. Copper conducted the heat more efficiently, but was more prone to dents than brass. Most copper cooking utensils were tinned on their working surfaces due to the risk of verdigris poisoning, but copper preserving pans were always left untinned as the use of sugar in quantity in the jam or jelly made the copper safe to use. There was also the fact that the tinned surface had a low melting point, only just above the boiling point of sugar.

As the pans were large and heavy, especially when filled with fruit, they either had two handles, one on each side, or could be carried by a swinging handle that fitted on to loops on each side of the pan.

The pans often had heavy use and examples can be found with sooty and grimy bottoms. These can be cleaned by using a proprietary brass cleaner, but it will often take a great deal of hard work and elbow grease. Never buy a pan that is very thin on its base; it will be prone to splitting.

Prices vary depending on the size of the pan and start at about £40–£80, with some larger pans costing £100–£250.

q

·QUILTS·&· ·PATCHWORK·

Quilted and patchwork bed covers have been made for generations. The earliest recorded patchwork is thought to be that belonging to an Egyptian queen in whose funeral tent a portion of patchwork ws found, made up of tiny pieces of dyed gazelle skin.

The craft of patchwork and quilting reached its peak in the 18th and 19th centuries and was especially popular in America where, it is said, a girl was expected to make thirteen quilts by the time she was married.

Quilts were made by sandwiching together a top and bottom layer of fabric, with a wadding of wool or cotton for warmth laid in between. The layers would be held together by stitching, and this was often done by placing the bed-sized layers on a large quilting frame.

Plain quilts would be enhanced with appliqué work or decorative raised stitching in a variety of designs, such as lattice patterns, baskets of fruit, plaits and waves. Certain patterns are associated with certain areas of the country. Welsh quilts would have hearts, pears and spirals worked on to them, while Durham quilts relied on straight bands of repeating patterns for appeal. Quilts from the Northumberland area show roses, feathers, shells and cable twists. Appliquéd quilts also followed traditional patterns, and traditional designs were given names such as the 'Tree of Life', 'Wreath of Grapes', 'Oak Leaf', or 'Birds in the Air'.

Patchwork quilts were also popular with the Victorians. These were made from scraps of fabric cut into various shapes, then stitched neatly and invisibly, although some decorative

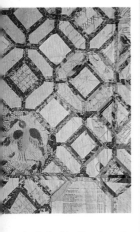

Back of the Georgian quilt (*BOTTOM RIGHT*), showing the use of bills, receipts and price lists etc as templates.

sewing was sometimes added in order to disguise the seams, using herringbone, feather or coral stitchery. Once the pieces were sewn together in sufficient quantity, the patchwork sheet was backed with plain fabric, layered with wadding, and quilted.

Geometric patterns, such as diamonds, triangles and squares, were used for the patchwork, with the hexagon being especially popular, and these shapes were sewn together in regular designs. Quilts having parallel bands or strips of different fabrics were called a 'strippy' and were made mostly in the North Country, England. The 'Log Cabin' design consisted of small rectangular strips of fabric joined together and arranged around a central square, with a contrasting square diamond pattern being created by a careful arrangement of the coloured material. Dark and light fabrics were combined to give the optical illusion that the same shapes were different, and careful shading could give a three-dimensional 'honeycomb' effect.

Some patterns were designed to radiate centrally. These could be made entirely of hexagons or other geometrical shapes which, when stitched together, could give a complex design having perhaps a floral effect. A design using squares arranged in a banded diamond pattern could achieve a striking effect by the use of bold

'Crazy patchwork' style Georgian quilt.

colours. Central star motifs were set in a square and had several banded borders, as did designs using petal shapes of varying sizes. Repeating patterns could be laid in dazzling three-dimensional blocks, or follow the fashion for the eight-pointed star, which was achieved by the clever use of elongated diamonds joined together.

In order to obtain the desired shapes in a regular size, templates were used. These were made of metal or thin card and were usually discarded once two or more pieces of fabric had been joined. Some ladies, however, used love letters as their templates and quilts have been found with these still in place. Large templates cut from newspapers have also been found.

The Victorian needlewoman could buy bargain 'bundles' of fabric and these were used for making 'crazy patchwork'. There was no regular shape to the pieces and no ordered design. Various materials were used, such as velvet, satin and silk, twill and cretonne.

Cottage quilts were made by using up odd pieces of calico or cotton print, perhaps from discarded dresses.

The condition of quilts and covers is important when buying. Small repairs can be carried out, such as the replacing of a patch or the mending of a small tear, but if the back of the quilt needs to be removed, this will destroy the quilting. It is best to avoid washing an antique quilt and it should be taken to a specialist company for dry cleaning.

Prices will vary according to age and condition, and whether the quilt or cover is hand sewn or machine stitched. An appliquéd quilt dating from the late 19th century will be from about £500 upwards; a patchwork quilt with a fairly basic pattern will be £200–£250.

Patchwork quilt in the 'Log Cabin' design, showing the optical illusion of light and shade.

·RADIOS·

Experiments in communication by means of electromagnetic waves were carried out as early as the 1880s by various eminent men, but it was the Italian Guglielmo Marconi who conceived a practical system of signalling by means of radio waves in 1897 when he exchanged messages across the Bristol Channel.

At first, the new system was used as a means of communicating or requesting assistance in shipping, before being used for military purposes during World War I. After the war, radio amateurs numbered many hundreds, and the demand for a broadcasting service grew. In 1922, the BBC opened by broadcasting the election results from Marconi House in the Strand, London.

By the 1930s, the wireless, so called because no wires were needed to connect one instrument to another, although wires abounded in the instrument itself, became an essential part of the British home. Technical progress had made obsolete the crystal set with its 'cat's whisker' detector, and the wireless soon became a piece of furniture. The loudspeaker and all the electronic components were housed inside the cabinet and this became the focal point for design.

Murphy Radios approached leading furniture designers such as Gordon Russell Ltd and they dominated the market with their plywood cabinets veneered in woods such as walnut, beech and bird's-eye maple. Designs followed fashionable trends and 'architectural' styles derived from the enthusiasm for all things Egyptian and Mayan (South American) were used, with cabinets also being designed in 'Jacobean' or 'Tudor' fashion.

'Lotus 3 valve AC All Electric Receiver' c.1930s with tulip motif on the speaker panel; £200–£250.

Radio receiver c.1930s (unmarked), showing the typical 'sunray' motif echoed in the graining of the wood in the cabinet, £200.

Apart from the cabinets, the grille that protected the loudspeaker was also stylishly made. Pye used a cut-out sunrise-and-clouds motif for their radios, A. C. Cossor featured a stylised flower pattern, while Ekco portrayed trees against a landscape in their large radiogram cabinets.

In about 1934, Ekco (E. K. Cole Ltd) produced the Ekco AD65, a radio with a Bakelite cabinet that was to revolutionise design. Previously, Bakelite cabinets had followed the 'furniture' style in having the plastic made to simulate wood grain, but Cole realised that Bakelite, capable of being moulded, was ideally suited to mass-production techniques. The Ekco AD65 was made in a round form in black Bakelite with chrome trim, having a semi-circular tuning scale in celluloid, and a round speaker placed centrally.

Radios from the 1930s are very collectable and prices can be high for those in Art Deco style. Those with wooden cabinets in a cubist design will be about £100–£250, while a radiogram such as the 1932 Ekco will be as much as £500–£1000. Bakelite-cased radios from this period will start at about £20–£50.

· RECIPE · & · · HOUSEHOLD · · MANAGEMENT · · BOOKS ·

Perhaps the most famous cookery book of all time is the *Book of Household Management* written by Mrs Isabella Mary Beeton in 1861. She died in 1865, aged 28, leaving a husband and two small boys. Her book has been revised over the years and reprinted in many forms, such as *Mrs Beeton's Everyday*

Selection of books;
£4–£25.

*Cookery, Mrs Beeton's All About Cookery
Book* and *Mrs Beeton's Family Cookery
and Housekeeping Book*.

The *All About Cookery* book
published in 1880 contains a heart-
rending memorial to Mrs Beeton, and
refers to 'her exquisite palate, unerring
judgement, sound common sense and
refined tastes'. By this date, the *Book of
Household Management* was being
published by Ward, Lock and Co., and
had run into its 279 000th edition. They
were also issuing *Mrs Beeton's
Englishwoman's Cookery Book* and
Beeton's Penny Cookery Book which was
available post-free for three-halfpence.
The books were illustrated with black
and white line drawings, with later
editions having lavish colour plates.

The books tell cooks how to roast
landrails (corncrakes) and make lark
pie, how to make jaunemange (a type of
egg and lemon jelly), gooseberry chips
(cooked, pulped, unripe gooseberries
cut into strips when dried), and how to
make a drink of toast and water.

Mrs Beeton was not the first to
compile a recipe or 'receipt' book, with
the *Experienced English Housekeeper* and
The Art of Cookery Made Simple both
appearing in the late 1700s. Authors
such as Mrs Marie Rundell, Dr William

Kitchiner, Eliza Acton and Alexis Soyer all published cookery books and in 1812 M. Appert published *The Art of Preserving*.

Part of the attraction of old cookery books are the advertisements such as Oakey's Silversmith Soap, Swinborne's Patent Gelatine, Goodall's Jelly Squares, Clarnico Cocoa, Lemco Beef Extract, Mazawattee Tea and Bumsted's Salt.

Cookery books from the 1920s and 1930s are also collectable, with such titles as *Lovely Food* by Ruth Lowinsky and *The Gentle Art of Cookery* by Mrs C. F. Leyel.

Manufacturers issued their own recipe booklets and leaflets. Food manufacturers such as McDougall's (flour), Oxo (meat extract), and Spry (cooking fat) produced recipes, as well as appliance makers such as Belling and English Electric (cookers), and Frigidaire (refrigerators).

Household management books were popular from the 1930s, with titles such as *The Concise Household Encyclopaedia*, *Household Management*, *Home Management* and *The Housewife's Book*, which were published by the *Daily Express*. These dealt with every aspect of home-making from washing-up to

Advertising pages of the books shown on page 129.

decorating, sensible shopping to getting rid of household pests. Other books concentrated on interior decorating, such as *Modern Homes Illustrated* and *The Daily Mail Ideal Home Book*, which was published annually. These give a fascinating insight into the style of houses and room settings, and the latest labour-saving gadgets. The books feature advertisements for items such as 'Housepoud' kitchen furniture, 'Lectross' the new electric clothes horse, the 'Easiwork' pressure cooker, and 'a laundry in a cabinet' from Hotpoint, which consisted of an electric cabinet washing and wringing machine, electric irons and electric clothes driers.

Most cookery books dating from the late 19th century and later can be found for under £10, with Mrs Beeton ranging between about £5 and £30, depending on the illustrations and the edition. Some books will be as little as £1–£2. Recipe booklets and leaflets are also inexpensive and a representative collection can be built up quite cheaply for as little as 50 pence to £1 per booklet on average, although rare or unusual examples might cost as much as £5.

Household management books will start at about £5, depending on the age of the book and the number of illustrations. Two-volumed encyclopaedias will start at about £10.

· REGISTERED ·
· DESIGN ·
· MARKS ·

In 1842, the Designs Act gave protection to manufacturers who registered their designs with the Patent Office Design registry in London. The diamond-shaped registry mark was used

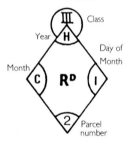

on goods where appropriate and each class was given a different number:

1. (I)   Metal
2. (II)   Wood
3. (III) Glass
4. (IV)   Earthenware (ceramics)
5. (V)   Paper-hangings
6. (VI)   Carpets

Classes 7, 8, 9, 10 and 11 (VII, VIII, IX, X, XI) included various textiles.

Three years' protection was given to Classes 1–6 (I–VI), provided the articles were made wholly or chiefly of the categorised materials.

The registered diamond was marked with the class of goods, the day, the month and the year of registration, and the parcel or bundle number. The original diamond was changed in 1868, so that the date letters appeared in a different place. A key to both diamonds is shown below:

REGISTRY DIAMOND
FOR 1842–67

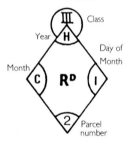

Index to year letters for 1842–67
(year letter at top)

A	1845	B	1858	C	1844
D	1852	E	1855	F	1847
G	1863	H	1843	I	1846
J	1854	K	1857	L	1856
M	1859	N	1864	O	1862
P	1851	Q	1866	R	1861
S	1849	T	1867	U	1848
V	1850	W	1865	X	1842
Y	1853	Z	1860		

REGISTRY DIAMOND
FOR 1868–83

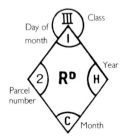

Index to year letters for 1868–83
(year letter at right)

A	1871	C	1870	D	1878
E	1881	F	1873	H	1869
I	1872	J	1880	K	1883
L	1882	P	1877	S	1875
U	1874	V	1876	X	1868
Y	1879				

The letter W was used as the year letter from 1st to 6th March 1878.

r

Index to month letters
(for both diamonds)

A	December	H	April
B	October	I	July
C	January	K	November
D	September	M	June
E	May	R	August
G	February	W	March

The month letter R was used between 1st and 19th September 1857; the letter K was used for December 1860. From 1st to 16th March 1878 the letter G was used for the month.

· DESIGN ·
· REGISTRATIONS ·

In 1883 the Patents, Designs and Trade Marks Act amalgamated all the categories in which glass, ceramics, metals, and so on, were grouped together into Class 4, and registered in a numerical sequence; this system was put into operation in January 1884. The manufactured article was marked with a series of numbers which were sometimes accompanied by the prefix Reg No. or Rd No. These numbers will give the date of registration of the design and will also, in most cases, identify the manufacturer. Records are held at the Public Record Office in Kew, Surrey, and are available for reference.

Design registration numbers from 1884

1884	1	**1885**	19754
1886	40480	**1887**	64520
1888	90483	**1889**	116648
1890	141273	**1891**	163767
1892	185713	**1893**	205240
1894	224720	**1895**	246975
1896	268392	**1897**	291241
1898	311658	**1899**	331707
1900	351202	**1901**	368154

·ROLLING· ·PINS·

These have been variously made in wood, glass, pottery and porcelain, and have been in use since the 17th century. Solid glass or ceramic rolling pins were initially the ideal medium for rolling pastry, being both cool and heavy; but they were also fragile and prone to damage. In the 19th century, wooden pins were favourite.

Glass rolling pins originated in the Nailsea area, near Bristol, and were made of pale green crown window glass, or of dark green bottle glass, although colours such as dark blue and black were also used, with opaque white and amethyst making a slightly later appearance. The rolling pins would be decorated with gilding, or enamelled with flowers, or mottoes, and some bore transfer-printed designs. Clear glass combined with loops of white, blue or pink glass in the Nailsea style were popular.

Glass rolling pins were initially tapered, rather than cylindrical, and had short 'knobby' ends. Some were hollow, with a stoppered end, and housewives used them as salt, sugar or tea containers, the contents being kept dry and also giving added weight when rolling.

Three advertising rolling pins.
FROM THE TOP:
Allinson's Wholewheat Flour, £20–£25.
Coomb's Eureka Flour, £20–£25. Both pottery.
A wooden rolling pin with Hovis marked on the handle, £10–£15.

Some glass pins were given as love tokens or sold as souvenirs. These were often too decorative for use and were hung on the wall by means of a beadwork handle.

Wooden rolling pins were made with short knobbed ends or long free-moving handles for ease of rolling. They could also be of tapered shape, used for rolling out a pie crust which needed to be thin in the middle, thicker at the edges. Scottish and Welsh oatmeal rollers were of cylindrical form, cut in deep concentric grooves. This gave the oatcake a ridged finish which allowed air to pass beneath it, giving it a lighter texture. Sone rolling pins had interchangeable, decorative 'sleeves', enabling the pin to be used for a variety of purposes, such as adding a patterned finish to shortbread.

Ceramic pins, originally made in Delft and Staffordshire pottery, made a revival in the 20th century, when manufacturers of various products used them to advertise their wares with appropriate slogans. Alternatively, the rolling pins could carry a printed recipe, issued by the maker of a particular brand of flour, for example.

Glass rolling pins will vary in price according to age and decoration. One in dark speckled glass will be about £40–£80 and one in a looped Nailsea style about £60–£120, while those decorated with mottoes, gilding or transfer-printed designs can cost from £100.

Wooden rolling pins dating from the 19th century and later start at about £10–£15, with those of decorative appearance, or having interchangeable 'sleeves', costing about £30–£40.

Ceramic pins from the 20th century with interesting slogans or recipes will cost about £15–£40.

· SAMPLERS ·

It is thought that samplers evolved as an aid to remembering or identifying the various decorative stitches and patterns used by a needlewoman. These 'reference' samplers were usually long, narrow strips of linen or fine canvas, being about 6 or 7 inches (15½–18 cm) wide, and as much as 30 inches (76 cm) in length, with the stitches worked in silk, woollen or linen threads.

By the beginning of the 18th century, the sampler was used less as a means of referring to embroidery stitches, and more as a teaching exercise in practising the art. The sampler therefore became more square in shape, until by about 1750, when the long narrow 'strip' or 'band' sampler had virtually disappeared.

Scholars and orphans learnt their numbers from samplers; they were taught how to spell by spending hours completing the alphabet and simple words in cross stitch. Religious texts, the Ten Commandments and the Lord's Prayer gave the children a spiritual education, while preprinted maps,

Religious sampler with a verse, showing Adam and Eve with the serpent twined around the Tree of Knowledge. Not signed or dated.

Detailed sampler made in 1912 by Sarah Ann Roake, aged 11.

which they outlined in simple stitching and framed with a floral design in more complicated stitches, gave them a lesson in geography. Mending was taught by the use of darning samplers which could be additionally decorated with floral sprays and baskets, garlands and ribbons, all worked in darning with a stem stitch outline.

Some samplers were made by using cut-work, drawn-thread and faggoting techniques, while others of a more advanced nature show the needlewoman's skill in dress-making with examples of hemming, buttonholing, seaming, tucking and gathering.

Buildings were a popular theme for decorative samplers, with cottages, castles, windmills and 'Solomon's Temple' all being carefully depicted. Adam and Eve and the Tree of Knowledge were other favourites.

Victorian samplers were made using a coarser linen than before, and with thicker Berlin wool being used in place of the fine wool thread or silk previously used. By about 1850, fine sampler work had largely died out.

When buying samplers, it is important to check the condition. Due to their age, they are rarely perfect, but

Sampler made by Hanah (sic) Russell, aged 13, in 1724.

those that have obvious damage, or are
frayed or worn, should be avoided
unless the repair work is minor.
Samplers should never be washed
without first checking with a specialist
or a museum for advice. If framing a
sampler, use an acid-free backing board
and mount with the same board to keep
the sampler from touching the glass.

Prices will vary according to age and
pattern, and whether the sampler is
framed or not. Unframed examples are
cheaper but, again, check for any wear if
the sampler has been folded repeatedly,
or for any length of time. A simple
sewing sampler will be about £25–£35,
one showing the alphabet about £70–
£100. A well-designed sampler will start
at about £300–£350.

· SCALES · & · · WEIGHTS ·

Domestic kitchen scales of the Victorian
era were usually of two types: the
beam-like scale with weights which
counterbalanced the item or goods to be
weighed, and the spring balance scale
which operated a pointer on a marked
dial showing a scale of weights.

The beam-like scale consisted of a
sturdy cast iron base with a weighing
pan set on a columned support on one
side, and a flat platform, also supported,
to take the weights on the other. The
pan was made of brass or base metal and
could be round or scoop-shaped,
although the latter is more often found
with the larger scales used
commercially. Butter and cheese were
weighed on beam-like scales that had a
round, flat weighing 'plate' or tray made
in white or marbled porcelain. Avery
scales often had a marbled plate
stamped 'Wedgwood' and these were
attractively marked with grey veining.

Spring balance scales
weighing up to 25 lb
(11.3 kg); £20.

The spring-balance scale made its appearance in the early 1900s when Salter produced an upright model made in cast iron or steel. A thin sprung column with cruciform arms supported a round shallow pan made in base metal, seldom in brass, and the circular dial was of brass or white enamel. G. Salter & Co. was the major manufacturer of these scales, and they were often marked with the company name. Other, inferior scales usually had a weighted tin-plate base.

When buying beam-type scales, ensure that the weights are all present and correctly graduated, although sets of these can often be bought separately. The brass pan should not be too badly dented or scratched, but the dirt and grime of years will give way to rigorous polishing with a good quality proprietary brass cleaner.

Spring balance scales should be accurate, and these can be tested with a known weight. Salter have reproduced their cast iron scales with a brass or enamel dial, so care should be taken when buying. Any cast iron base that has been painted by a previous owner can be dealt with by using a good

Scales with a dished pan for weighing fruit and berries, ¼ oz–2 lb (7 g–907 g); £30–£35.

S

Butter scales having
a round ceramic pan,
1 oz–2 lb (28 g–907 g);
£60.

quality paint stripper and then buffing
the metal to a fine black finish with
grate polish, which is available from
most ironmongers.

Tin-plate scales will cost about £15–
£30, those with a cast iron base will be
about £40 or more. Brass pans add to
the cost. Dairy scales with a flat ceramic
pan and accompanying weights cost
from about £20–£30.

The weights that accompanied the
scales were made in brass or cast iron
and varied between a massive 56 lb
(25.4 kg) used commercially to a tiny ¼
ounce (7 g).

Brass weights were of different types.
The bell weight was upright, waisted
and had a carrying handle on top.
Another type was cylindrical, having a
small integral knob on top. Stacking

Weights ranging between
1 oz (28 g) and 1 lb
(453 g); £8–£15.

weights were flat circular weights, recessed for placing on top of each other in order of size.

Cast iron weights were also made as stacking weights, or could be round and bun-shaped. Others resembled a square pyramid with a flat top, having an attached ring for lifting.

Cup weights, usually made in brass, were contained in a lidded holder, the base being narrower than the top. The weights were designed to fit snugly into one another, and the smaller weight was half the weight of the one it fitted into. The lidded holder weighed twice as much as the weights it contained.

If not sold with the scales, weights will cost about £10–£15 for a set in circular cast iron; similar ones in brass will be about £10–£30. Brass bell weights start at about £80–£150, more if marked with a maker's name. Sets of cup weights will cost from about £50–£70, but check that the smallest weight is not missing.

(See also LETTER SCALES & BALANCES.)

· SEWING ·
· MACHINES ·

In 1790, Thomas Saint of London patented a machine for sewing leather but it was almost a hundred years before his idea was fully exploited. In about 1875/6, Newton Wilson of Birmingham found the expired patent and made a working model which used chain stitch. Others, both on the Continent and in America, had also been experimenting with the idea of mechanical stitching, with Barthelemy Thimmonier producing a wooden factory machine in 1829, and in 1845 an all-metal machine. Elias Howe of Massachusetts produced a rough but working model in 1839 and,

Table top sewing machine marked 'Willcox & Gibbs Sewing Machine Co. New York. London. Paris'. c.1880–95 (Hastings Museum).

after going into partnership with George Fisher, brought out an improved model using lock-stitch in 1845, and another in 1846.

But it was not until 1850, when a German-born American, Isaac Merritt Singer, produced his 'Singer's Perpendicular Action Sewing Machine' that it became viable for the domestic market, although it was primarily intended for use in the factory.

Singer's was the first machine which could cope with sewing straight, curved and angled seams in a continuous fashion, and was operated by means of a treadle or foot pedal, leaving the operator's hands free to deal with guiding the fabric.

In 1858, Singer manufactured his 'Family' or 'Turtleback' machine, but this proved unsuccessful due to the lightness of construction. Between 1859–65, he developed his 'Transverse Shuttle – Letter A' machine which had a boat-shaped shuttle which moved from left to right, rather than forwards and backwards as before. The shape and design of Singer's machines became the prototype for all sewing machines that followed. Both treadle and table models were made, with the 'Singer New Family' machine introduced in 1865, available in both styles.

The sewing machine was expensive to buy – Isaac Singer set up a system of hire purchase in 1856 – and therefore worthy of decoration. Cabinets were made of polished wood and treadle machine cabinets were equipped with several drawers for holding thread, spare needles and so on. The stand and treadle were generally made of cast iron and were ornately cast in a variety of designs, and sometimes gilded. The machine was japanned in black and was inlaid with mother-of-pearl and/or lavishly gilded in floral or leaf patterns and scrolled arabesques.

When buying, it is important to check the condition of the sewing machine. The bobbin and shuttle are often missing and these can be difficult, if not impossible, to replace. Penetrating oil will free the moving parts and rust can be dealt with by using a rust remover and careful use of very fine steel wool. Machines with the gilded decoration intact are more desirable, but any missing gilding should not be touched up as this will affect the machine's

Singer sewing machine with gilded transfer decoration. Model no. Y7472947.

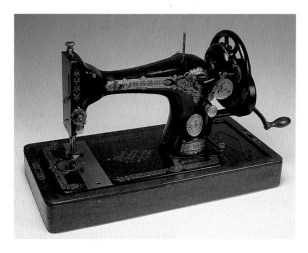

historical worth. Machines from the
1920s/1930s generally had a top-fitting
carrying case which slotted into the
base. Check that this is a good fit and
that the key, if present, works smoothly.

Table top machines dating between
1880 and 1930 are still freely available
at auctions and can be bought for as
little as £10–£50. Much of the price
depends on the maker, the condition of
the machine and the amount of
decoration. Treadle machines can be
found fairly cheaply from about £30–
£100 upwards. Very early machines are
regarded as museum pieces and are
rarely available to the collector.

· SHAGREEN ·

This is generally recognised as the
untanned skin of sharks or other large
fish which was dyed green, red or black
and used for covering the small cases of
precious objects such as medallions,
snuff boxes or watches, and also for
covering the cases of more practical
items such as spectacles.

However, *Lloyd's Encyclopaedic
Dictionary*, dated 1895, gives an added
definition: 'A species of leather or
parchment, prepared without tanning
from the skins of horses, asses and
camels. The strips, having been
softened by steeping in water, and
cleared of hair, are spread on the floor
and covered with the seeds of the
Goose-foot. A covering of felt is laid on,
and the seeds are pressed into the skin
by trampling or mechanical means, thus
producing the peculiar granular
appearance of shagreen. It is dyed green
with sal-ammoniac acid and copper
filings, red with cochineal, &c.'

The dictionary goes on to add:
'Shagreen is also made of the skins of
otters, seals, sharks, &c.'

· SHEFFIELD ·
· PLATE ·

In the early 18th century, the only
method of making items with a finish
that imitated silver was to coat them
with silver foil, a method called close
plating (q.v.). This proved
unsatisfactory, however, as the silver
coating often blistered and lifted,
revealing the iron or steel below.

In 1743, Thomas Boulsover (or
Bolsover), a Sheffield cutler, discovered
that if a sheet of silver was fused on to a
thicker sheet of copper, the two would
roll out evenly when put through a mill.
Articles could therefore be made which
resembled silver but at far less cost.
Bolsover soon discovered that the new
metal was capable of being hammered,
rolled or drawn into wire without any
shift between the copper and silver.
However, he did not fully exploit his
discovery, confining his manufacture to
such things as buttons and small boxes.

In the 1750s Joseph Hancock, also of
Sheffield, began to use the new
material, producing candlesticks, coffee
pots and saucepans. Matthew Boulton of
Birmingham also mastered the new
technique and in 1762 began production
in his Soho factory. By 1770, he was the
largest single manufacturer of the new
Sheffield plate, as it was now called.

Sheffield plate can be fairly easily
recognised. Early plate was silvered on
one side only and the interior surfaces
were tinned to prevent verdigris
poisoning from the copper; this tinning
was never carried out on electro-plated
articles.

Items were always die-stamped from
the sheet metal, and never cast. This
gave a lightness of weight to the pieces
compared to those made in silver or that
were electro-plated. Where the surface

Late 18th-century tea
caddy in Sheffield plate.

of the plating is worn, the copper base shows through, and this is known as 'bleeding'. Because of the composition of the copper mix, it shows up as rather brown, as opposed to the red or pale brassy tones which show through on electro-plated pieces.

Later replating of Sheffield plate can be detected if examined carefully. The silver used in the process was of sterling or .925 standard, but replating techniques involve the use of pure silver. As this is of a different colour from .925 silver, any replating should be visible.

· SMOKING ·
· ACCESSORIES ·

Ever since tobacco was introduced into Europe at the end of the 15th century, smokers have needed many accessories to make their habit more comfortable and many of these now make attractive collectables.

ASHTRAYS

These were made to cope with the ash from cigars, which had been introduced into Europe early in the 18th century. Cigar smoking reached England about 100 years later and soon became popular. One of the earliest references

Ashtray and cigarette holder set by Royal Winton (Grimwades) in a lustre finish; £25–£40.

Group of Noritake
(Japanese) ashtrays and
cigarette holders;
£30–£80.

to an ashtray occurred in about 1857
when it was referred to as an ash-pan.

Ashtrays were made in pottery and
porcelain, glass, silver and various
metals. They could be large, small,
plain, decorative, commemorative, of
novel design or issued by manufacturers
for advertising purposes.

Souvenir ashtrays were made in great
quantities during the 19th century.
Some had a facsimile pipe, cigar or
pocket watch incorporated into the dish.
These bore the name of the resort or
mottoes such as 'Husband don't annoy
your wife'.

Small oval ashtrays dating from the
1920s were set with a seated lady
dressed in a suitably modest bathing
suit. Some novelty ashtrays were
combined match or cigarette holders,
adorned with humorous animals such as
spotted cats or dogs. The cigarettes or
matches were placed in a series of short,
raised, hollow columns set on each side
of the animal. Other combined ashtrays
had an oblong projection on to which a
cardboard matchbox would be fitted.
When pushed down over the projection,
the inner box was forced up, revealing
the matches. Most souvenir and novelty
ashtrays are marked 'Foreign' and are

usually of German origin, although Japanese ashtrays were also imported in large numbers.

Glass or brass ashtrays were fitted into wooden or metal smokers' stands. These tall columned receptacles were intended for use when sitting down, being at just the right height for the smoker to flick his ash into the waiting container.

Glass was also used, set into a miniature replica of a car tyre. These ashtrays date from around the 1920s/1930s, although some are still being made today, and they were issued by tyre manufacturers such as Michelin and used for promotional advertising purposes. The tread on the tyres is faithfully reproduced in miniature.

Prices range from about £5 for the tyre ashtrays, about £7–£10 for those with amusing spotted animals. Bathing belle ashtrays are about £18–£25, with souvenir and commemorative ashtrays starting at about £10, but the price will rise according to attractiveness and rarity.

CIGARETTE LIGHTERS

Friction matches (see MATCH HOLDERS and VESTA CASES) put an end to the use of tinder boxes and these were used for the lighting of cigarettes and cigars until the beginning of the 20th century, although a 'lighter' had been devised as early as 1807. This was the 20-inch (51-cm) high 'Temple of Vesta' designed by C. F. Schutz which was operated by means of an electrically charged resin disc. The spark that was produced ignited the hydrogen gas, which then flamed out of the mouth of a lion crouched at the base of the temple.

The first Dunhill lighter was made in 1923. It was called the 'Everytime Lighter' as it was so reliable, but later

Group of 1940s lighters;
£2–£10.

became known as the 'Unique' lighter.
Dunhill, amongst others, also produced
the popular 'touch-tip' watch lighters.
These were heavy table-top lighters of
square shape and had a working pocket
watch set in the side. Many lighters
were stylishly enamelled in black with a
chrome trim, and were operated by
means of a hollow rod stuffed with
petrol-soaked wadding. The rod was
withdrawn, then pressed down hard on
to another spring-loaded rod, and this
action operated a flint wheel, producing
a spark which lit the wadding. Smaller
watch lighters were made in the 1930s
by firms such as Ronson. They were
operated by means of a wheel and flint,
activated by a positive thumb action.
They were leather-covered and
intended for the pocket.

Some lighters were more decorative
than functional. The bronzed metal
figure of an Art Deco 'bat dancing girl'
some 11 inches (28 cm) high, for
example, would be set on a marble or
onyx base. The lighter itself took the
form of a hollow metal column which
had a long narrow striking plate and a
reservoir for petrol. The small rod which
was set into this column was wadded
and had a protruding disc-like flint.
When the flint was scraped along the

Art Deco 'Bat Dancer' cigarette lighter on onyx base; £120–£180.

striking plate, the resulting spark ignited the wadding.

Trench Art lighters were made during the war, with soldiers using scraps of brass, coins, bullets and shell cases.

Novelty lighters abounded in the 1930s. A Ronson 'touch-tip' table lighter featured a negro standing behind a black and chrome cocktail bar which was complete with shaker and glasses. Heavy chrome-plated lighters were also fashionable, and these were modelled as aeroplanes and skyward-tilting rockets. Golf and cricket balls, realistically produced, were popular at this time. It was also in the 1930s that Ronson brought out their 'Pencilighter', made of

Ronson 'Touch-tip' lighter with a watch set into the side; £150–£200.

chrome-plated brass and plastic, which incorporated a real pencil.

When buying lighters, it adds to the value if they are working properly, although small repairs can be made. Missing springs, however, can prove to be a problem and it can be a good idea to buy a 'lot' of old lighters at auction and cannibalise them for the repair of others. A touch-tip lighter should show a spark.

Lighters will vary enormously in price with small, plain pocket versions from the 1920s/1930s starting at about £10–£20. Named lighters such as Ronson or Dunhill will be more; some of these can be incredibly expensive, with gold Dunhill lighters costing £1500–£2000 and more. Dunhill also made the 'Lighthouse' table lighter which stands 24 inches (61 cm) high and weighs 110 lb (50 kg). It features a lighthouse made in 18-carat gold set on an island of amethyst and was sold at Christie's in the mid-1980s for £37 000. A pencil lighter from the 1950s will be about £35–£50, Trench Art lighters are about £10–£30 upwards. An Art Deco figural lighter will be about £150–£200, and the Ronson 'cocktail cabinet' lighter about £500–£700. Chrome-plated aeroplanes and rockets cost from about £60–£100, and table-model watch lighters start at about £100.

MATCH HOLDERS & STRIKERS

These are unlidded containers with a striking surface, usually roughened or ribbed, made for the safe storage of the volatile matches used in the 1850s. They were intended to stand on the desk, table or mantelpiece and were manufactured in pottery and porcelain, wood, metal, glass, papier mâché, ivory. Some resembled short spill vases, while

Carved wooden holder in the shape of an owl, with the head lifting off; £35–£40.

Brass 'Go-to-bed' match holder. The user would place a lighted match in the central hole at the top of the holder and place it on the washstand. This gave him just enough time to see his way to his bed before the match went out; £20–£25.

Mauchline ware holder and striker showing a view of the pier at Southend; £25–£30.

others were made in the shape of boots or shoes. There were holders with dished bases to take the spent matches, and ornamental examples with bisque figures standing in front or to the side of the cylindrical container. These featured children, jockeys, pedlars and street-sellers, fishermen, peasants and animals such as rabbits or frogs. Some were made in pairs with a girl holding a cat and a boy with a dog, for example.

Glass spheres were of threaded construction (for striking) and had a central hollow for the matches. These are often mounted with hallmarked silver rims (see HALLMARKS).

Advertising holders were made for use in taverns and public houses and they advertised drinks, cigarettes and tobacco. These could resemble beer barrels or bottles or have an ashtray incorporated.

With the advent of the matchbox and the safety match in the late 19th century, match holders were slowly superseded, until by the 1920s they had virtually disappeared.

When buying, it can be difficult to tell the match holders from the small Victorian spill holders. However, all match holders, whatever their style, had a roughened or ribbed section on which to strike the match, and this is an important means of identification.

Prices start at about £15–£25 for those made in pottery or porcelain; novelty ceramic holders will be about £30 upwards. Those in brass or metal start at about £10–£15.

PIPES

Pipe smoking was well established by the 18th century, with many smokers using clay pipes. Early examples were largely undecorated, although a few were cut with simple motifs around the bowl. The long 'churchwarden' pipe was introduced in the mid-19th century, but as it was almost 36 inches (91 cm) in length, it was soon phased out. The popularity of the clay pipe was threatened by the meerschaum pipe in about 1850 and manufacturers turned to making 'fancies' or 'fancy clay' pipes. These had bowls in the form of heads such as negroes, jockeys, statesmen or comedians such as Ally Soper and were varnished before making in imitation of meerschaum. Less fanciful pipes had bowls decorated with acorns, leaves, basketwork, ribbed patterns or sporting pastimes. The Scottish clay pipe, or 'cutty sark', had a stem which could be snapped or broken down to the length preferred by the user.

The meerschaum pipe is perhaps the most ornate type of pipe and the bowl is often intricately carved. Meerschaum is a white clay-like mineral and the word is derived from the German for 'sea-foam'. With use, the pipe became discoloured by the tobacco smoke and attained a mellow tone which ranged from yellow to almost black. Because the medium was capable of being easily carved, the bowl of the pipe became its most important feature; heads of people and animals, both fantastic and grotesque, were portrayed and these were sculpted

Churchwarden clay pipe made at the Broseley works.

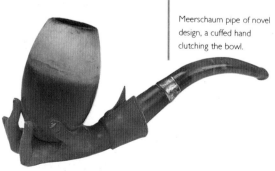

Meerschaum pipe of novel design, a cuffed hand clutching the bowl.

Meerschaum pipe with a carved bowl, amber mouthpiece and mounted with a silver band.

in fine detail. Other pipes had even more ambitious carvings, perhaps showing a girl clad in draperies looking rather like a ship's figurehead. The figure group of a stag being pursued and attacked by hounds was also depicted. More simple designs such as a hand or an eagle's claw holding the bowl were also popular. Meerschaum pipes, like clay, were absorbent and gave a cool, 'dry' smoke. They were usually fitted with amber mouthpieces.

Pipes made from wood such as cherry had also been made for some years, but these suffered from the drawback of carbonation and cracking. However, it was discovered that the heather root or 'briar' made an excellent pipe and by giving it a vulcanite mouthpiece in the late 19th century, the new pipe soon became extremely popular with smokers. As the briar-root was so hard, it was turned on a lathe rather than carved, and was given a silver mount for decoration. Some novelty pipes were made, using vulcanite for the decorative sections. For example, the head of W.

Briar pipe with silver band.

G. Grace, the cricketer, was moulded in vulcanite and set with a briar bowl; a vulcanite leg could be seen kicking a briar football (the bowl).

Pipes will cost from about £10–£20 upwards for a clay pipe, about £50–£100 for a well-styled briar pipe with silver banding. Cased meerschaum pipes will start at about £200, and those with extravagant carving will be about £500–£1000 and more.

VESTA CASES

Friction matches were first made in about 1826 and consisted of wood coated with a poisonous yellow or white phosphorus. Workers were at risk during manufacture and suffered 'fossy' jaw, a disease caused by the chemical and the fumes. By the 1830s a match with a less phosphorous head had been produced, and by the 1850s small waxed vesta matches, sometimes known as 'lucifers', were in use. The new matches were successful but volatile, and were prone to accidental ignition. The small pocket vesta case was devised and remained in use until the advent of wooden matchboxes.

Most vesta cases were under 2 inches (5 cm) in length, and were usually of square or rectangular shape. They had a hinged lid and a ribbed striking section on the base, and some had a ring or loop for attaching to the watch chain. Mostly made in silver, they were also available in silver-plate, gold, brass, base metal,

Silver vesta case with a pattern of engraved ivy leaves. Hallmarked on both parts of the case, Chester 1901.

LEFT: Brass vesta with striker on top and hinged at the back; £20–£25.
RIGHT: Silver-plated vesta with hinged top and striker on the base; £15–£20.

Bakelite vesta case c.1890,
having a flip top and
featuring a cricketer;
£45–£50.

Hallmarked silver vesta
case with foliate pattern.

wood and plastic. The cases could be
fluted, engine-turned, embossed or
engraved in a pattern of scrolls, acanthus
leaves, flowers, or could be enamelled
with sporting scenes, dogs, the facsimile
of a playing card or a tastefully draped
reclining nude.

Novelty vestas were made in the
shape of hearts, a lady's corset, pigs,
tortoises, a horse's head, violins,
miniature books, suitcases, boots,
horseshoes and a bottle of wine.

Simple vesta cases should be
hallmarked (see HALLMARKS) and this is
usually stamped on the inner rim. Avoid
any silver-plated pieces that are worn or
yellowing, and ensure that enamelled
cases are free from chips.

Prices will be from about £25–£45 for
silver vestas with engraved or embossed
decoration and about £50–£100 for
novelty examples made in base metal
either gilded or silver-plated. Vestas
made of plastic, such as vulcanite, will
be about £20–£40 upwards, depending
on the moulded embossing.

· STONEWARE ·
· JARS ·

The making of jam, chutney and potted
meat or pâté was an everyday part of the
Victorian housewife's duties, and she
chose to store her produce in glazed
stoneware jars. The jars could be
sterilised before use, as they were
capable of withstanding boiling water;
they remained popular until after World
War II.

Until the 18th century, the jars had
sloping sides, being wider at the top
than at the bottom; these were known
as 'galley pots'. After this date, jars
became straight-sided and had a
shoulder below the rim to take the
string that held the cover tightly in

Four stoneware jars.
Height 8 in–15 in
(20.3 cm–38 cm);
£8–£20.

place.

With the advent of transfer printing in the pottery industry in the late 19th century, jars were made specifically for preserving companies, who were quick to take advantage of the advertising possibilities. Doulton & Watts (now Royal Doulton) supplied Crosse & Blackwell, for example.

Perhaps the most frequently found jars are those made for James Keiller & Sons of Dundee, who made marmalade. The company was established in 1797 and used the same type of stoneware jar until 1940. W. P. Hartley's jams were sold in straight-sided jars which had parallel grooves cut vertically into the clay. The name of the company was impressed into the base, sometimes with a lighthouse logo that was their trademark. Jars marked 'Aintree' date from 1886–1900; those marked 'Aintree and London' date from 1900. Frank Cooper's marmalade was contained in stone jars from 1874 until the mid-1920s.

Stoneware jars from the early 20th century can be found for about £2–£8. More unusual jars such as 'Cairns Fairyland Jams' will be £15–£25; while 'R. Swift's Celebrated Ormskirk Brawn', showing a pig's head in blue, will be about £35 upwards.

· TABLE · LINEN ·

With the advent of industrialisation in the late 19th century, embroidered tablecloths were mass-produced quickly and cheaply. Use of the sewing machine (q.v.) meant that hems could be tackled easily and the machine-made lace sewn on with hardly any effort.

However, these advances did not stop the Victorian housewife from wanting to make her own linen or cotton tablecloths, and these were made using whitework embroidery, drawn-thread and cut-work techniques.

Whitework embroidery consisted of using white thread on white fabric and, although coloured threads were becoming popular, many women preferred the plainer style. The pattern was given a raised effect by padding or by the use of satin stitch. Flowers, stems and leaves were carefully depicted.

Drawn-thread work involved many patient hours of work. Selected threads were pulled out of the fabric in sections to form a pattern. Some threads were left isolated, which were then tied together for more interest. The resulting pattern was often geometric in appearance and a cloth might be edged

Doily or table mat using tape lace and drawn threadwork.

Drawn threadwork tray cloth; too many drawn threads, however, have made the cloth very prone to snags.

with a border of both square and triangular designs.

Cut-work meant the use of scissors. The pattern was designed and small sections of fabric were then carefully cut away. The raw edges were carefully sewn with fine, neat stitches. Occasionally, coloured threads and silks were used for this neatening process.

Wide crocheted lace borders could be added to finish off the tablecloth. The lace could be made of cotton thread, which gave a rather coarse and heavy appearance, or could be more delicate with the use of fine silk thread. The depth of the edging varied between 1 and 5 inches (2½–12½ cm) and could have a shell-shaped finishing edge, or be worked into deep 'V' points. Cloths were also made with inserted borders of lace.

When buying table linen, condition is all-important, especially if it is to be put to use. Check carefully for tears or holes; these can be expensive to have repaired professionally. Check for stains by holding the cloth up to the light; avoid rust and mildew stains as these are virtually impossible to remove.

Cloths can be washed and will sometimes benefit from an overnight

t

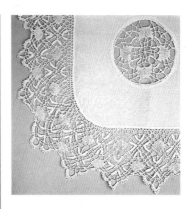

Delicate crochet work used to edge a tablecloth and as circular inserts at each corner.

soak in a mild detergent, but avoid the use of bleach as this will damage age-weakened fibres. A dip in starch will improve the appearance of the tablecloth. Those with whitework embroidery should be ironed from the back so that the embroidery is not flattened but stands out in relief.

Hand-embroidered cloths are more expensive than their machine-made counterparts and it is important to learn to recognise the difference. Machine-made stitches are more regular than those sewn by hand, as is the lace that might border the cloth.

Prices will vary according to the size and design on the tablecloth. An afternoon cloth with lace edging will be about £25-£50; a large cloth for the dining table will be about £75 upwards.

· TEA · CADDIES ·

Tea drinking was popularised in England by the wife of Charles II in the 17th century. It was an expensive drink and available only to the very rich. By the 18th century it was being drunk more widely, but was still costly. To prevent the servants helping themselves, the tea was kept locked in a caddy, the word coming from the Malay 'kati', meaning a unit of weight of just over one pound. Tea was imported from China in porcelain jars.

Although porcelain caddies were made, they were fragile and silver therefore became popular. Wooden boxes were also favoured and these were divided into two compartments, one for black tea, the other for green. Those with three compartments would have a small bowl, usually of glass, for blending or mixing the tea. The tea caddies, also known as tea chests and tea caskets, were made in wood such as rosewood, mahogany, walnut, maple and satinwood or were covered with shagreen (q.v.). Other materials included mother-of-pearl, tortoiseshell and papier mâché. The boxes were often lined with pewter or antimony to keep the tea fresh.

A George III tea caddy in rosewood will cost about £200–£250 upwards; one of the same date with marquetry decoration and two secret drawers will cost £1250 and more. Victorian tea caddies are more affordable and a two-compartmented caddy in rosewood will be about £150–£180; one of fairly plain design in mahogany will cost about £60–£100.

Tunbridgeware tea caddy with a view of Bayham Abbey on the lid.

· TELEPHONES ·

The American, Alexander Graham Bell, is generally credited with the invention of the telephone in 1876, although

Skeleton type telephone c.1895. It has no dial as it was used via an exchange and received its power from the generator seen at the side (Hastings Museum).

experiments had been carried out since about 1861. In 1878, Bell established 'The Telephone Company Limited' in London, with Thomas Edison, a rival American, coming to England the following year and setting up the Edison Telephone Company. The two companies joined forces in 1880 as the United Telephone Company.

In 1880, the Post Office opened its own exchanges while other companies which had sprung up operated under licence, eventually amalgamating into the National Telephone Company. By about 1914, however, the Post Office had taken over completely. The first public exchange was opened in 1912, with automatic exchanges being introduced in the 1920s.

The 'skeleton' telephone was introduced in about 1895 and was in production until about 1930. The telephone was in glossy black with gold transfer patterns, and had a vaguely 'sit up and beg' appearance. It had a central turret and black curved legs which concealed the magnets for the hand generator and the induction coil. The handset with its large curving earpiece was set down on an ornate brass cradle of candelabrum shape.

This was followed in about 1900 by

the 'candlestick' or pedestal telephone of columnar style. The mouthpiece was at the head of the column, with the baton-like earpiece being held by two grips at the side. The dialling mechanism, added later, was housed in the base. It, too, was in use until the 1930s.

The handset telephone of traditional shape was introduced in 1929. It was the first all-plastic telephone and was originally made in mottled brown Bakelite, although black soon became standard, with jade green, Chinese red and ivory being available by special order. A sliding celluloid tray (known as a 'cheeseboard tray') with dialling instructions was fitted at the base of the telephone. A telephone with an in-built bell was introduced in 1936, and this model was of a heavier, more square shape. It, too, had a 'cheeseboard' tray.

In 1959, the 700 series was launched. It marked the end of the standard black telephone, as the telephone now became available in a range of colours, with two shades of grey being popular in offices. The brown rayon twisted cord was replaced for the first time by the 'curly' extended cord.

It is possible to buy old telephones that will work on the present telephone system. These can be bought in working order from reputable dealers, or can be converted at specialist shops for about £15–£20 upwards. The date of the phone is often printed on the handset. Some of the early skeleton-type phones are being reproduced, so care must be taken when buying.

A skeleton telephone will cost £100 and more, as will a candlestick telephone. Handset phones from the 1930s and 1940s will start at about £25–£40 for those in black, about £50–£100 upwards for coloured models.

tiles

Tile making has been known in Britain since the 12th century when tiles were used as flooring in churches. But perhaps it is the Victorian tiles that offer so much variety to the collector. In 1830 Samuel Wright, a Staffordshire potter, patented a new process for the manufacture of 'ornamental tiles, bricks and quarry tiles'. The firm of Minton bought a controlling interest in the process and began manufacture of the new encaustic tiles in the 1840s.

The inlaid tiles were made by pressing plastic clay into a patterned mould. When the tile was turned out, and after drying, coloured liquid clay or slip was poured into the moulded indentations. After further drying, the surface was smoothed, and the tile fired. These tiles were known as plastic-bodied tiles.

Another important development in the 1840s was the process of clay dust pressing. This had been invented by Richard Prosser, who used it for making clay buttons, and once again Minton bought a share in the patent. However, by the late 1900s, most companies were making tiles by this method. The powdered clay was moistened and then pressed between two metal dies by means of a screw-press, thus creating the pattern. The drying period was short and this reduced production costs. The tiles were then fired, before being decorated, coloured and glazed. Plain, smooth-surfaced tiles were often decorated with transfer-printed designs.

Tile making boomed from about 1870 with many artists and designers becoming involved. Minton (now split into two separate companies: Minton Ltd and Minton Hollins & Co.) lost their monopoly, with firms such as Maw & Company, who had taken over Worcester's share of Wright's patent, competing for business. William De Morgan, an artist and designer, established a pottery in Cheyne Row, Chelsea, and began making tiles, using red clay from Poole in Dorset. Copeland and Garrett (later known as W. T. Copeland) used transfer-printed patterns on tiles as well as making encaustic tiles, and these resembled those used on plates. Other manufacturers include T. & R. Boote, Malkin Edge, Pilkington's and, briefly, Wedgwood.

The Arts and Crafts movement and the Art Nouveau style influenced tile designs, and artists like Burne-Jones designed panels such as 'Beauty and the Beast'. Walter Crane produced some exquisite designs for Pilkington's, and the company won an award in 1898 for their decorative, hand-painted majolica tiles. Tiles were decorated with flowing patterns in both transfer printing and relief moulding. Some tiles were tube-lined, where the clay was contained in a kind of 'icing bag' and squeezed out in thin lines. Large scenic panels were popular. Some depicted characters from nursery rhymes or showed a stylised tree. Gordon Forsyth, also of Pilkington's, designed a superb panel showing a Persian gentleman lying at ease in a tree-lined garden.

Two Art Deco tube-lined tiles by Pilkington c.1930s; £15–£20 each.

Brown and white transfer-printed tile, marked Mintons China Works, Stoke-on-Trent.

p.165

TOP: Two tiles having stencilled designs. The one on the left by Maw & Co. (£10–£12), the other by Craven Dunhill & Co.; £5–£7.
BOTTOM: Delft tile in blue and white; £12–£15.

Three Minton tiles with patterns of stylised flower heads; £5–£12 each.

tiles

Group of Victorian tiles in majolica and transfer-printed designs; £4–£10 each.

Two Art Nouveau tiles showing stylised flower heads.

Tiles were also designed in pairs or series, such as 'Night' and 'Morn' which show a fox and a bat outlined against a crescent moon and a night sky, and a crowing cockerel against the rays of the morning sun, with the fox slinking away. Maw & Co. produced 'Children's Pastimes', a set of six tiles which were transfer printed in grey/brown on a cream background. William Wise designed sets of engraved tiles for Minton. 'Animals of the Farm' consisted of twelve tiles, each showing a different animal such as pigs at a trough, sheep lying down, shire horses, cows in a stream and so on. Wedgwood released a twelve-tile series featuring the months of the year, and 'November' shows a fisher lad walking barefoot along the edge of the sea, a creel on his back.

Photographic portrait tiles made a brief appearance in about 1897. These were produced by Sherwin & Cotton, J. H. Barrett &

Co., Minton, and Craven Dunhill. The tiles were moulded in relief from a photographic reproduction from gelatine. The majority of tiles featured well-known statesmen such as David Lloyd George or notables such as General Booth of the Salvation Army. The monochrome glaze could be red, green, turquoise blue or sepia.

Tiles are often marked on the back with the maker's name, either impressed or in relief, and this can be an aid to dating. Occasionally, a registered design number appears (see REGISTERED DESIGN MARKS) which also helps to establish age.

Tiles are readily available and need not cost a fortune, although panels designed by known artists are now museum pieces – a large William De Morgan tile panel was sold at a London auction in December 1989 for £42 000. An Art Nouveau majolica tile with a stylised relief pattern will cost between £10–£40; a tube-lined tile from the 1930s showing an Art Deco-style landscape will be about £10–£20, although a single tile designed by an artist/designer such as Charlotte Rhead, and signed, will cost over £150. Transfer-printed tiles will start at about £5 each. An upright 'run' of fireplace tiles will be about £30–£60, and a set of six 'Series' tiles by Minton will be between £120–£150. Photographic tiles are about £50–£70, depending on the subject portrayed; a rare Sherwin and Cotton tile by George Cartlidge will be about £150–£250.

Various Delft tiles in blue and white, showing river and landscape scenes; £20–£25 each.

· TIN · OPENERS ·

The idea of preserving food by first heating it, then sealing it hermetically, was conceived in France by Nicholas Appert in 1809. An Englishman, Peter Durand, took the process a step further in 1810 when he patented a tin-plated iron or steel container that would contain heat-sterilised food. However, the method was not developed commercially until about 1812 when the firm of Donkin and Hall established a cannery in Bermondsey. By 1830, tinned food was widely available, although it was expensive to buy, and the large 7 lb (3 kg) tins almost impossible to open. The lids were sealed with solder, and the tins came with printed instructions to 'cut round on the top near to the outer edge with chisel and hammer'.

Tin openers soon made their appearance, and early models intended to cope with tins of bully.beef (corned beef) were made in cast iron. A bull's head was popular, with the cutting blade

Varied selection of tin openers, the two at the bottom of the illustration having bull heads; £2–£15.

forming the jaw and emerging as a spike for piercing the tin on top of the head. Some spikes were separate from the cutting blade, however. There was no body, but the bull's tail curved around on itself to form a handle. This design carried on well into the 20th century.

Plainer tin openers followed with the advent of the double-sealed ridge can, and these had wooden handles. The rotary opener was introduced in the 1930s.

A bull's head tin opener will cost about £12–£15; wooden-handled openers are cheap at about £2–£5.

· TINS ·

These come in many different shapes and sizes, and were made for a huge variety of goods. Biscuits, sweets and chocolates were packed in novel containers (see BISCUIT TINS).

Cigarettes such as Capstan Navy Cut were contained in round cylindrical tins, Player's Navy Cut were neat in a square flat tin; other brands include Gold Flake, Gold Leaf and Murray's Mellow Smoking Mixture.

Tiny tins were used for pen nibs or for gramophone needles (see GRAMOPHONES), and it is thought that there are over 400 different varieties of the latter with Columbia and Edison Bell being collectable names.

Commemorative tins were issued for royal events; Cadbury's produced a tin commemorating the silver jubilee of George V and Queen Mary, while Brock and Company, who manufactured fireworks, issued a tin for the same occasion which showed the royal couple amidst a shower of fireworks.

Royalty put their names to tins during times of war. A small chocolate tin was sent to the fighting forces during the

Small match holder or vesta case, advertising Bournville Cocoa by Cadbury's; £7–£8.

Tins of all sizes; £2–£25.

Boer War which showed a profile portrait of Queen Victoria and bore a message in a facsimile of her writing which read, 'I wish you a happy New Year'. Soldiers in World War I were sent a brass-lacquered metal tin at Christmas 1914. It was provided by the Sailors' and Soldiers' Christmas Fund, a charity organised by Princess Mary, the daughter of George V. The tin's contents varied, but usually tobacco, cigarettes, a pipe, sometimes a lighter, a photograph of Princess Mary and a Christmas card were placed inside. The lid showed Princess Mary in profile, and embossed plaques bearing the names of the Allied nations.

Other World War tins contained medicated lozenges and a card from Victory V Gums, chocolates from the British Grocers' Federation, and cigarettes from the YMCA (Young Men's Christian Association).

Collectable tins should be in good condition, with the paintwork not defaced, the hinges sound, and the tin not too battered or dented.

Prices vary according to size and rarity. Gramophone needle tins can still be found for £2–£5 upwards; sweet and toffee tins start at about £7–£10, although a bucket-shaped tin with a handle from Sharp's will cost about £50–£60. Cigarette tins can be about £20 upwards, with a Rattler tobacco tin costing £35–£50. Commemorative tins are about the same price, and a 'Princess Mary's' tin will be about £20–£25 minus contents.

Hinged chocolate tin made for Cadbury Bros. Ltd. showing three dogs and entitled 'Three British Queens'; £7–£10.

· TRIVETS ·

The earliest of these were three-legged circular or triangular pot stands which supported the cauldron or cooking pot in the fire. The three legs splayed out evenly, and adjusted to the irregularities of the floor of the grate which would be covered with layers of ash and embers. The three legs were more stable than a stand with four legs.

Not all trivets stood in the fireplace, however; some stood at the side and were used to take the boiled pan of water or simmering stew when removed from the heat. These were often

Three brass trivets; £20–£35.

ornamental and made in cut steel or cast in brass in attractive openwork patterns and designs.

With the advent of the barred grate, trivets were made with the three legs as before, plus an extra leg, sometimes two, that hooked over the bars of the grate. Some of these trivets also had a handle for ease of use when hot.

Trivets were used to take hot containers in other parts of the house, too. Specially shaped trivets with three stubby feet were used to support the sizzling flat irons (see IRON STANDS) when they were taken off the heat of the fire. Four-legged trivets were used in the dining room. These were known as footmen, and kettles, hot dishes or bowls of piping punch were placed on them for the hostess's use. They were often made in brass with attractive cutaway patterns.

Trivets will cost about £10 for a round cast iron pot stand with short stubby feet. A brass Victorian trivet will be about £25–£40 upwards, with footmen starting at about £50–£70.

Group of cast-iron trivets; £7–£15.

u

· UMBRELLAS ·
· & · PARASOLS ·

Both umbrellas and parasols have been
used since about 1000 BC when they
originated in Egypt and were used only
by royal personages. They could also be
found in Assyria, Persia, China, Greece,
Rome and Japan, and formed part of
religious rituals in Africa and India.
Credit for the invention of the
collapsible umbrella goes to the
Chinese, whose emperor used them in
about 25 BC.

However, they went into a decline in
Europe with the fall of the Roman
Empire and were not revived until the
16th century, when the Italians used
them, calling them an 'ombrello'. They
reached France in the 17th century, and
were called a 'parasol'. By the 18th
century the parasol was being widely
used in England, although umbrellas
and parasols were not differentiated
until the 19th century.

The use of an umbrella by a
gentleman was frowned upon until the
Prince Regent, influenced by
everything that was Chinese,
popularised them. When a gentleman
by the name of Jonas Hanway dared to
use one in the 1750s, he was lampooned
and caricatured.

Early parasols were made in fine
fabrics such as Indian muslin, silk or
satin, often hand-painted with floral
designs, or embroidered with feather
stitch and decorated with fringing or
wide bands of hand-made lace. The
handles were often ornate, made in
mother-of-pearl, tortoiseshell, rhinoceros
horn or carved ivory, and were
sometimes additionally decorated with
ribbons and bows in velvet, satin or silk.

In 1844, the 'La Sylphide' automatic
opening parasol was patented by

Two umbrella handles.
LEFT: A curving drake's
head.
RIGHT: A small carved
parrot.

An umbrella concealed within a walking stick. 'The Paragon' made by S. Fox & Co. Ltd.

William Sangster. Taffeta was now a popular fabric, with cotton being used for cheaper umbrellas. The ribs were made of whalebone.

Fashions changed quickly on the umbrella scene. The pointed pagoda style was popular in 1860, only to give way to domed parasols with striped covers. Polka dots were all the rage in the 1880s, competing with the oriental-style parasols. Many parasols were lined with lace or a contrasting material in order to hide the unsightly ribs.

Men's umbrellas in the early 19th century were usually of cotton or silk, with handles of horn or ivory. They were untidy and unwieldy when folded and many men shunned their use until Samuel Fox patented his 'Paragon' frame in 1852. This gave the umbrella a lightness and strength it had formerly lacked. The introduction of metal 'cups' that held the ribs in place enabled the umbrella to be tightly furled, making it more manageable.

When buying umbrellas and parasols, check the condition of the fabric carefully as this can rot with age and damp. Most wear appears at the rib tips. Rolled umbrellas have often faded

Parasol with inner frills of black lace. The wooden handle is painted and decorated in gold and pink, and embellished with a fabric bow.

Folding parasol in cream
silk and with a carved ivory
handle.

where they have been exposed to
sunlight and are spoiled by unsightly
pale stripes.

Victorian parasols will start at about
£20–£50, although some can cost £50–
£100. Oriental-style parasols, made of
oiled paper, will be about £10–£20.
Umbrellas will also be about £20–£50,
but much depends on the style of the
handle.

· UMBRELLA ·
· STANDS ·

Umbrella stands had two purposes: to
display the decorative parasols when not
in use, and to catch the drips from a wet
umbrella after the rain.

Victorian stands offer great variety.
Perhaps the simplest were those which
consisted of a column headed with four
large metal rings into which the
umbrella was slotted. The octagonal tray
caught the drips and protected the floor.
Cast iron stands were often very ornate
with a pierced and patterned back plate
on to which the oval supporting sections
were fitted. The base was tray-like and
sometimes additionally had a pottery
container. Novelty cast iron stands
featured figure animals or, appropriately,
frogs, and some of these were painted.
Huge cast vases were imported from the

A 20th-century cylindrical
umbrella stand made in
sheet brass, stamped out
in a pattern of revellers at
an inn; £45–£50.

An oak hall umbrella stand with quadrant top and green painted drip tray; £38–£43.

Far East and these were decorated with piercing and relief work.

Bamboo umbrella stands were open in design and were fitted with a painted metal tray. Wooden stands, made in dark oak, also followed this open style and had barley twist supports. Larger stands would have tiled or embossed copper back panels.

Brass stands were also made, some in the style of those in bamboo and oak, or they could be of simple cylindrical form. The latter were made of sheet brass, and were often heavily embossed.

The cylindrical, tube-like form was adopted in earthenware, too, with Burmantofts Pottery of Leeds producing them in brilliant colours.

Umbrella stands are still useful today and are therefore collectable. A large Art Nouveau stand with a tiled or copper back plate will be about £250–£350; a smaller stand with barley twist or bobbin-turned supports will be £50–£150. Pottery stands will cost about £100 upwards, depending on the design and the factory. Cylindrical Victorian brass stands will be about £50–£100.

· VACUUM ·
· CLEANERS ·

Until 1901, the only aid to carpet
cleaning was the carpet sweeper (q.v.)
patented in 1853. Cecil Booth worked
on the theory that air was sucked into a
vacuum, taking with it dirt and dust. If
the air could be filtered out again,
leaving behind the debris, it would be a
boon to housewives. However, the first
vacuum cleaner he produced was too
large to fit into any normal household
and was soon nicknamed the 'Puffing
Billy'. Undeterred, he established the
British Vacuum Cleaner Company and
hired his machine out, together with a
team of men to operate it. In 1904, the
company brought out a smaller vacuum
cleaner that could be plugged into a
light socket and used by the domestic
staff of the household.

Other companies soon realised that
there was a potential market and
brought out their own versions, but it
was not until about 1908 that the
familiar upright bag and stick vacuum
made its appearance. The idea had been
patented by an American, J. M.
Spangler, who had demonstrated it to
W. H. Hoover. Hoover, quick to realise
that Spangler had a winner, set up the

'Mary-Ann' 2-way electric
cleaner, plus accessories,
made by British Electric
Domestic Appliances.

Hoover cleaner c.1920 marked 'It beats as it sweeps as it cleans'.

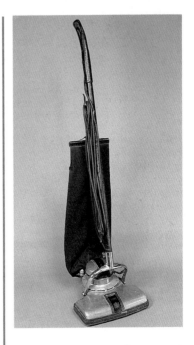

Electric Suction Sweeper Company and began manufacture. By 1912, the cleaners were being exported to England, and soon Hoover's product was known worldwide.

In 1926, the cleaner was refined by the addition of a rotating metal bar which led to the adoption of the slogan, 'It beats as it sweeps as it cleans'.

The cylinder vacuum cleaner appeared in about 1910, and was fitted with a disposable bag in the 1930s.

Despite the limited appeal of vacuum cleaners, they can be expensive, with an early cylinder model costing up to £100. Upright cleaners will also reach similar high prices if early, but as there are very few specialist dealers, it very much depends on where the vacuum cleaners are bought. Car boot sales and flea markets are ideal hunting grounds.

· WALKING ·
· STICKS ·

The Victorian gentleman would
consider himself less than well dressed
if he promenaded without a walking
stick. From about 1850, the fashionable
stick was the Malacca cane. This was a
lightweight stick made from the stem of
a palm tree, with a grip-type handle
made of gold, silver, ivory or horn, the
latter often being silver mounted. Some
sticks had ball or knob grips, with the
crook-handle not making its appearance
until the end of the century, and
becoming popular in the 1920s.

Handles were intended to give
interest to walking sticks. Animals and
birds were often featured, and one can
find sticks surmounted by a horse's
head, a Staffordshire bull terrier, and a
realistic owl. These were carved in
wood, sometimes cast in silver and often
had eyes set with glass or semi-precious
gems.

Novelty walking sticks were all the
rage with the Victorians. Sword sticks
were carried for protection, and the oil-
fired lamp stick gave illumination in the
dark streets. Racegoers would carry a
stick containing a boxwood rule for
measuring the height of horses, the
fisherman concealed a rod in his, while

Three silver-mounted
walking sticks; £20–£35.

TOP: Cane stick with crook handle; £12–£15.
CENTRE: Walking stick cut from a branch; £12–£15.
BOTTOM: Twisted stick with carved animal head handle; £25–£30.

men of a curious or enquiring nature could buy a stick fitted with a telescope or a spy glass. Canes fitted with watches, compasses, tobacco pipes, corkscrews, glass flasks and tiny drinking glasses were all readily available.

Novelty sticks should be examined carefully, as the hollowed-out cavity is prone to splitting. Check the handles; umbrella handles can sometimes be substituted for the original.

Prices for novelty sticks can be as high as £500–£1000, especially those with unusual additions such as watches. Ornate-handled sticks will be about £100–£200 upwards, depending on the style and material of the handle. Plain walking canes with silver ends will start at about £25–£50.

TOP: Elegant walking stick dating from c.1830, formerly used by the Duchess of Kent.
BOTTOM: Carved whalebone stick.

·WARMING· ·PANS·

Heated containers for warming beds were essential in the chilly British winters, and by the 16th century the warming pan had come into being. Until the Victorian era the warming pan was of a traditional shape, and consisted of a large pan (rather like a frying pan) with a hinged and pierced lid that was set on a long handle. The pan was filled with hot embers from the kitchen fire, then carried upstairs to the bedroom where it was inserted between the bed sheets and moved around until the bed was thoroughly warm. After use, the warming pan was taken back downstairs, emptied, and then hung on a hook near the fireplace, ready for the following night.

Early warming pans were made of iron, 16th-century ones of brass. Copper was not used until the 18th century, as the impurities in the metal caused cracking, risky when carrying hot coals. In 1728, a method of machine-rolling copper sheets was perfected, and copper warming pans became popular. The long iron handles, often as much as 3 feet (1 m) in length, were eventually replaced by cast brass, later by wooden handles.

Brass warming pan with decorated lid.

Early pans had a large deep bowl, but this became smaller and shallower after about 1750. The shape varied slightly, too, with early pans having flat lids and straight sides, becoming curved with domed lids from the 18th century.

Seventeenth-century pans were decorated with embossing and piercing, with the holes arranged in a circular pattern. By the mid-1800s, the piercing had become extremely ornate, and resembled lacework or coarse filigree. The 17th century also saw finely traced

Copper warming pan.

designs executed in shallow engraving.
Stars, flowers and foliage arranged in a
series of tiny dots were popular.
Hammered relief patterns were also
common, and these could sometimes be
very complex.

Water-filled warming pans were
introduced towards the late 1700s, and
had a screw top to make the pan
watertight set either side or on top of
the upper surface. By the beginning of
the 19th century, the handles were
detachable and by about 1820 they had
virtually disappeared.

Care must be taken when buying
warming pans. They revived in
popularity in the 1970s and many
reproduction pans were made. These
are generally lighter in weight than the
old pans, and are shinier. The riveting is
also modern. Replacement handles need
not affect the desirability of the old
warming pans, but they should cost less
than their complete counterparts.

Copper and brass warming pans with
little decoration will cost about £50–
£100; those with elaborately chased or
embossed designs will be £100–£250,
and those with intricate pierced designs
will start at about £200.

· WATCH ·
· STANDS ·

A pocket watch was a precious object to the Victorian gentleman and, when removed at night, would be placed carefully in a purpose-made stand. This would often be set on the night table, enabling the watch to double as a clock.

Watch stands were made in an incredible variety of shapes and sizes, and in materials such as silver, silver-plate, cast iron, brass, wood, mother-of-pearl, papier mâché, pottery, porcelain, glass and Bakelite. Fabric watch pockets that hung at the bed head were embroidered or decorated with beadwork.

Stands in brass or iron were ornately cast in Gothic style, or could have elaborate winged panels. The watch was placed in a 'pocket' at the back, the face showing through a circular cut-out. A cast jaguar-like animal could hold the watch by means of a hook between his

TOP: Large watch stand carved with acanthus leaves, roses and thistles. Height 11 inches (28 cm); £150–£200.
LEFT to RIGHT: Sycamore watch stand with velvet-lined recess; £60–£90. Ormolu and glass box with silk lining; £60–£90. Bellows-shaped stand with a carved eidelweiss flower; £30–£50.
Hand-painted papier-mâché stand; £25–£50.

TOP: Ebonised watch stand made in imitation of a longcase clock; £100–£150. *LEFT to RIGHT*: Brass stand with enamel decoration in an Oriental design; £50–£80. Mauchline ware box with transfer decoration; £40–£60. Cast metal jaguar on marble base; £100–£150.

teeth. Another novelty stand would depict a street light with revellers below. The tiny bulb set in the lamp was battery operated and illuminated the watch that hung below.

Brass was also combined with glass to create square or oval shallow boxes with a sloping lid. The watch rested on silk and was magnified by the glass cover.

Wood was used extensively and could be carved ornately in various shapes. The most utilitarian stand in wood consisted of a round holder with a velvet-lined hollow for the watch, standing on a turned stem and having a circular base. An easel-style stand folded in on itself, doubling as a watch case. This type was usually Swiss, made as souvenirs and carved or chiselled in various patterns that often included the edelweiss flower. More elaborate wooden boxes were made in rosewood with ivory banding and brass studs on the lid. An interior cut-out section took the watch and this could be lifted at an angle for display purposes. Some watch holders resembled miniature longcase clocks, others represented the Coronation throne with a hook on the back of the chair for the watch. When a cushion on the seat was lifted, it revealed a money box (q.v.).

Pottery and porcelain stands were extremely ornate. A Coalbrookdale stand would be garlanded with relief flowers, a bisque stand would have Bacchanalian cherubs supporting a ring of vines and grapes. Staffordshire watch stands were large and usually showed two or three figures painted in orange and cobalt blue. The ceramic pocket at the back held the watch.

Papier mâché and porcelain souvenir stands were often simple in design, consisting of a board-like stand, fitted with a hook to hold the watch.

Silver stands could resemble photograph frames, and had heavy scrolled embossing. The watch would rest against a velvet lining. Silver was also combined with mother-of-pearl, with a shell to take the watch chain or fob set on a delicate silver stand, the watch hanging from a scrolled frame above.

Some small clock cases are sometimes marked up as watch stands, but the

TOP: Staffordshire watch stand with three figures, decorated in orange and cobalt blue; £80–£150.
LEFT to RIGHT:
Coalbrookdale stand with a scenic panel; £100–£150.
Metal and ceramic stand, hand-painted, with a tray for the watch chain or albert; £80–£100.
Bisque (unglazed porcelain) stand with supporting cherubs; £60–£90.

aperture which would have taken the clock movement is far too deep for the slim pocket watch. Brass and cast iron stands have been reproduced, so buy carefully.

Prices start at about £30 for a watch stand on a turned wooden column and for a flower-painted papier mâché example. Ivory-banded boxes will be about £80–£120. Cast iron stands will cost about £45 upwards, depending on size. Brass will be about the same price. Pottery and porcelain watch stands will be about £30–£40 for a simple souvenir variety, Staffordshire figure group stands start at about £80–£100, but ornate porcelain watch stands, such as Coalbrookdale, will be about £150–£200. Silver stands are expensive, much of the value being in the weight of the silver, as well as the ornateness of the design, but they will generally start at about £80–£120 upwards. Glass stands will start at about £60–£80.

· WEIGHTS ·
See Scales & Weights

· WICK ·
· TRIMMERS ·
*See Candle Snuffers &
Wick Trimmers*

· WICKER ·
· BASKETS ·
See Baskets, Wicker

glossary

ALLOY: Mixture of metals.

ANTIMONY: Bluish-white element, sometimes combined with lead to make an alloy.

BAKELITE: A plastic made from phenolic resin, discovered by the Belgian chemist Leo Baekeland in 1907.

BALUSTER: An elongated pear shape on a short column or pillar, as in a banister on a staircase.

BARLEY (SUGAR) TWIST: Turning a column in a spiral to give a twisted effect.

BELL METAL: An alloy of copper and tin.

BISQUE: Unglazed porcelain, also known as biscuit.

ERASS: Alloy of copper and zinc.

BRIGHT CUTTING: Kind of engraving on silver giving reflected light from the bevelled facets, so achieving additional brightness.

BRITANNIA METAL: An alloy of tin, copper, brass, antimony and bismuth (q.v.).

BRONZE: Alloy of copper and tin.

BRUYÈRES: The heather root used for making briar pipes.

CASEIN: Plastic made in imitation of ivory, pearl and tortoiseshell.

CELLULOID: Semi-synthetic plastic made from cellulose nitrate.

CERAMICS: All types of fired clay.

CHINOISERIE: European imitation of Chinese decoration.

CLOSE PLATING: A coating of silver fused on to an article made of iron or steel (q.v.).

COPPER: Basic material used in making brass and bronze.

DRIP PAN: Wide rim on a candlestick to catch the drips.

EBONISED: Inferior wood stained to resemble ebony.

EBONY: Dense, hard black wood.

ELECTROPLATE: Items coated with a deposit of silver by an electrolytic process (q.v.).

EMBOSSING: Relief decoration.

ENGRAVING: Where the pattern is cut out with a graver.

EPNS: Electroplated nickel silver.

ETCHING: Where the pattern is achieved by the use of acid.

FINIAL: Ornamental top to lids.

FUSED PLATING: Another term for close plating.

GUNMETAL: Alloy of copper and tin.

IVORINE: Plastic made in imitation of ivory.

JAPANNING: A method of varnishing wood, metal and papier mâché with a heat-resisting lacquer.

JAPONAISERIE: European imitation of Japanese decoration.

KNOP(PED): A term used in glassmaking to describe a knob of glass used decoratively, as on the stem of a wine glass.

LIGNUM VITAE: A very hard wood from South America.

LOZENGE: Diamond pattern with a long horizontal axis.

LUCIFER: Type of early match.

glossary

MAUCHLINE WARE: Small items made in sycamore wood and decorated with scenes done in pen and ink or transfer printed.

MEERSCHAUM: Type of pipe; mineral used for pipe making.

MOTHER-OF-PEARL: The iridescent layer inside a shell used decoratively.

NICKEL SILVER: Alloy of copper, zinc and nickel.

NOZZLE: Part of a candlestick into which the candle is placed.

PAKTONG: Alloy similar to nickel silver, made in China.

PAPIER MÂCHÉ: Moulded paper pulp which hardens when dry.

PEWTER: Alloy of tin, lead and copper.

PIERCING: Fretwork decoration.

POKERWORK: The art of putting designs on light-coloured wood by scorching with a heated steel point.

RECEIPT: Old term for a recipe.

RELIEF: Design which stands out from the surface.

SCONCE: Back or supporting plate for a candle holder; socket used to hold candles.

SCROLL: Curving or spiral decoration.

SEPIA: A brown pigment; of brownish colour.

SHEFFIELD PLATE: Items made of a combined sheet of silver fused with one of copper.

SPELTER: Alloy composed mainly of zinc.

STEEL: Alloy of iron and carbon.

STERLING SILVER: Silver with copper added.

TRANSFER PRINTING: Method of printing whereby the pattern was etched on to copper plates before being 'transferred' to the item to be decorated.

TREEN: Word used to describe small articles made of wood; household utensils made of wood.

TRENCH ART: Articles made by soldiers during the two world wars.

TUNBRIDGE WARE: Small wooden items decorated with inlaid mosaic veneer, made at Tonbridge and Tunbridge Wells.

VESTA: Type of early match.

VENEER: A thin slice or layer of quality wood glued on to the surface of another wood to give a superior finish.

VULCANITE: A hard vulcanised rubber.

WARD: Part of the key which activates the locking mechanism.

WROUGHT IRON: Iron hammered into shape and not cast.

index

index

index

· ACKNOWLEDGEMENTS ·

The appeal of a book can often be affected by the quality of its photographs—sometimes to its detriment. However, *Household Treasures* does not fall into this category, as all the items illustrated have been superbly photographed by Peter Greenhalf, A.R.P.S— and I am most grateful for his expertise.

I must also extend my gratitude to the experts, friends, colleagues, and collectors who have given freely of their time and advice, as well as allowing me to borrow items of interest for photography. I would like to express my thanks to the following:

Roger Barclay of Barclay Antiques, Little Common, Bexhill, Sussex; Dave J. Barker; The Gramophone Shop, 31 John Street, Luton, Beds; Victoria Williams, Curator of the Hastings Museum and Art Gallery, Hastings, Sussex; Steve at the Luton Antiques Centre, John Street, Luton, Beds; Auriol Miller; David R. Miller; Sue and John Moore (the 'potty' people); Barry Muncey; Pamela & Barry Auctions, St Albans; and Tim Rice at the Luton Antiques Centre, John Street, Luton, Beds.

Last, but by no means least, I would like to thank Ann Lingard and the staff of Rope Walk Antiques, Rye, Sussex, without whose patience, help and expertise this book would have been sadly lacking.

Muriel M. Miller